KU-169-225

GAINSBOROUGH

GAINSBOROUGH

Stephen Butler

STUDIO EDITIONS

LONDON

First published in Great Britain in 1992
by Studio Editions Ltd
Princess House, 50 Eastcastle Street
London W1N 7AP, England

Reprinted 1993

Copyright © 1992 Studio Editions Ltd

The right of Stephen Butler to be identified as the
author of this work has been asserted by him in
accordance with the Copyright, Designs and
Patents Act, 1988.

All rights reserved. No part of this publication
may be reproduced, stored in a retrieval system,
or transmitted, in any form or by any means, electronic,
mechanical, photocopying, recording or otherwise,
without the prior permission of the copyright holder.

ISBN 1-85170-856-1

Printed and bound in Hong Kong

INTRODUCTION

In considering the life and work of Thomas Gainsborough a curious paradox quickly becomes apparent. Although quite a substantial amount of written 'evidence' about him survives, he remains a tantalizingly enigmatic personality. We have, for instance, more than one contemporary or near-contemporary biography, a great number of his own letters and business papers, the tributes and memoirs of contemporary artists and critics and, due to his place among the most fashionable and the leading intellectual circles of his day, many casual references to his daily life in various diaries and memoirs. But for all his great success and ubiquitousness it must not be forgotten that what we now understand by the term 'biography' – quite apart from related concepts such as 'personality' and 'character', 'genius' and 'artist' – is very different from the scope and application of these same words during the late eighteenth century. This is not the place to analyse this generic problem of historiography; let us just say that we are faced with a great deal of information that fails to tell us in a direct way what we now consider we need to know.

This, of course, is frequently the case in dealing with historical figures both more ancient and more recent than Gainsborough. But in the case of this artist many commentators have been forcefully struck by it because of the quite extraordinary transformations that are periodically apparent in his work. Scholars, forced to rely to an unusual extent on the often ambiguous biographical and autobiographical information which survives, have sought parallel upheavals in his personal life and circumstances. This is sometimes at the expense of a sensible appraisal of the cultural and social forces influential upon Gainsborough's career, as conclusions as to his motivation and psyche are extrapolated in a quite cavalier manner from what are often little more than anecdotal titbits. It has to be said that this approach is tempting, because what we can discern of Gainsborough's personality points to an unusually attractive and engaging man, a man, moreover, who would make a fascinating subject, were such a thing possible, of a modern psychological biography. In the end any examination of such a subject needs to balance the personal and familial with the socio-cultural influences on his or her work.

What we do know for certain about Gainsborough is that he was an outwardly sociable, quick-witted, garrulous, generous, intelligent and promiscuous man. He seems to have been held in special regard because he was admired and liked as a person as well as being fêted as a great artist. On the other hand we can glimpse – little more – a troubled personal life, and we have reason to suspect that to some extent he was a man who 'wore a public face' to mask the emotional trauma not least of mental illness in his immediate family and perhaps even in himself. A man, too, who felt deeply uneasy about his role in society, and his ability to play it. His movements and actions are clear; his motivations and inner, emotional life far less so.

Alongside his contemporary Sir Joshua Reynolds, Gainsborough stands at the forefront of a great renaissance in British painting. It could be argued that where Reynolds's career – not least because of his influence on the nature of academic institutions – paved the way for the rich succeeding tradition of Academic painting which was disrupted in the late nineteenth century by the onset of Pre-Raphaelitism, Gainsborough provided the impetus for the parallel development of naturalism and the realist landscape tradition of Britain and France. In Britain his revivification of landscape painting was of immense significance, as Constable, its greatest practitioner, acknowledged. But it was primarily as a portraitist that Gainsborough was acclaimed throughout most of his life, an irony compounded by the fact that his portrait technique had little or no influence on the work of later artists.

Both Gainsborough's and Reynolds's mature work can be seen as attempts – though very different ones – to encompass the two great conflicting influences in British culture at that time: broadly, Classicism and Romanticism. To their contemporaries the approaches of the two men seemed radically opposed, but in truth their art was in many ways more similar than they or their supporters would have cared to admit. And there is no doubt that each recognized and admired the abilities of the other despite at times an open hostility between them. Reynolds, if one cares to make odious comparisons, undoubtedly had the greater influence – more profound and more lasting – on both the organization of the British art establishment and the course of European art as a whole. Indeed, he was one of the very few British artists in any age to have a significant impact on the development of art on the Continent; Gainsborough did not. Reynolds, despite some lamentable weaknesses in his basic technique and occasional lapses of taste, was much the more imaginative and daring of the two. On the other hand, Gainsborough's landscape work, largely unrecognized until quite late in his career, provided the foundations of a peculiarly British tradition, which was developed by Constable and Turner and survives, albeit half-submerged beneath more recent ideological influences in art, to this day. And his

portraiture, despite its eccentricity, has come to be recognized as among the most brilliant of any age.

For all their differences, there is a certain symmetry to the lives of Gainsborough and Reynolds. Both were born in the deep countryside; Gainsborough in Suffolk and Reynolds four years earlier in Devon. Both were gifted with an ability to assimilate and transform the art of previous ages into work that was at once new and assured. Both were businessmen with an eye to the main chance of the contemporary market; indeed it could be said that between them they made acceptable the idea of the professional artist in Britain. Both perceived the possibility of an art that stood on equal terms with music, drama and poetry and fought for the recognition of painting as a worthy subject for the same kind of critical debate and cultural approbation.

Reynolds, who had schooled himself in the Classics and in the neo-classical art of Italy and France, was intellectual and didactic by temperament, at home among the great scientists and men of letters of his age. His trenchant and revolutionary views on the proper schooling of artists and on the fit subjects for art masked an often surprisingly weak grasp of the rudiments of mixing and applying paint, with the result that for all their daring and bravura, many of his works are now in a sorry condition. Gainsborough, on the other hand, though possessed of an astonishing ability to learn both quickly and completely, had little education in the formal sense and was neither a theoretician nor an intellectual. He boasted of his lack of familiarity with the Classics and with contemporary thought, rarely read a book, and preferred the company of actors and musicians to that of writers and intellectuals.

He did, however, have one gift that Sir Joshua sadly lacked: a complete sense of his own limitations. He never attempted anything beyond the capacity of his lively, yet self-confessedly undisciplined mind. It could never be said of Gainsborough's work that it is

Lady Sarah Bunbury Sacrificing to the Graces,
by Sir Joshua Reynolds, 1765.
Oil on canvas, 242 × 151.5 cm
The Art Institute of Chicago

in the least pretentious. Alas, the same is not true of Reynolds, whose classical and mythological flatteries have come to be seen as faintly ludicrous beside Gainsborough's straightforward, though glamourous approach. It is possible, of course, that Reynolds, who was far from humourless, regarded such works as *Lady Sarah Bunbury Sacrificing to the Graces* as ironic comments on the vanity of his aristocratic clients; unfortunately, there is sufficient evidence to

suggest that such hyperbole seems to have been as much his idea as theirs.

There is another similarity between the two, perhaps the most important of all, and that is that both used the lucrative business of society portraiture to finance their more personal artistic interests. In Reynolds's case this was History painting – works representing Biblical, mythological or historical scenes, often with an allegorical gloss. This was then accepted as the highest form of painting on the Continent, and Reynolds brought it to similar prominence in Britain. For Gainsborough, landscape painting fulfilled the same role, though the genre was held in such low esteem both in Britain and abroad during his formative years that this devotion is in itself one of the most curious things about him. In the process, almost as it were by accident, as both men displayed opinions about the drudgery of 'phiz-mongering' that veered between boredom and deep loathing, they raised the standard and the standing of portrait-painting to an unprecedented level.

Thomas Gainsborough was born in 1727 in Sudbury, Suffolk, and was baptized in the Independent Meeting-house in Friars Street on 14 May. The day of his birth is unknown, but in an age when a very high percentage of children failed to survive infancy, it was usual for christenings to follow quickly after the birth. There is no record of Gainsborough celebrating his birthday during his life; perhaps he himself did not know it.

His parents, John Gainsborough and Mary Burrough, themselves Suffolk-born and -bred, were relatively well off, though the family business – John was a clothier and wool merchant – was in decline at the time of Thomas's birth. He was the fifth son, one of eight eventual children. He would have grown up in a close-knit community surrounded by aunts, uncles and cousins in an area where his family was on friendly terms with – and more than likely related to – almost every other family in their class.

In the eighteenth century, family ties were both stronger and in some ways weaker than they are today. Stronger in that it was not at all unusual for cousins, grandparents or in-laws to share the family home; looser in that this often meant that children grew up with as much if not more contact with these relatives as with their natural parents. Social convention dictated that marriages were as often arranged as not, and girls in particular might find themselves conveniently wed to comparative strangers in the curiously businesslike and unsentimental manner of the times. Whether John and Mary Gainsborough married for love is not nown; Thomas did, against his parents' wishes, and had some cause to regret it. As a successful painter he remained in close contact with his seven siblings, and provided considerable financial support to them, notably to his older brother John, known as 'Scheming Jack', an inventor whose thirst for knowledge was matched only by his signal lack of financial acumen.

From his petit bourgeois Dissenting background, Thomas inherited strong religious convictions: surprisingly, despite his thoroughly hedonistic outlook, he regularly went to chapel all his life and refused to work on Sundays. He also made a number of close friends among the priesthood. One of his brothers became a minister, and one of his sisters married one. There is nothing to indicate that this religious background was a stern or cramping influence on his development. Indeed, he seems to have enjoyed a thoroughly liberal regime as a child and to have been positively encouraged in his ambitions by his parents.

Of Gainsborough's childhood little record has survived, though there are the usual charming anecdotes with which the early days of the famous are embellished. It is said, for instance, that at the age of six or seven he could forge his father's handwriting well enough to be let off his studies at Sudbury Grammar School, where his uncle, the Reverend Humphry Burrough, was headmaster. By his own admission he played truant as often as not, preferring to go fishing or sketching in the fields. All his life Gainsborough insisted that he had little or no learning, though he was an inveterate collector of books and had by the end of his life acquired a fine library. He was also a brilliant letter-writer. His assessment of his own intellectual abilities may have been self-deprecating and without false modesty, but his contemporaries took a different view, and it may be that his lack of self-confidence was masked by a quick brain and a ready wit. By all accounts he was the most entertaining of speakers, able to hold his own in any company.

Nowadays we tend to regard the pre-industrial countryside in which Gainsborough grew up as an almost Arcadian haven of peace and tranquility. In this interpretation we are influenced by the landscape art of the period, and of later figures such as Constable, and encouraged by the imagery of poets such as Thomas Gray, Oliver Goldsmith and William Wordsworth. In actuality, the late eighteenth century was a period of immense and irrevocable change in the British countryside, of social strife goaded by political and technological pressures. These, as we can see in retrospect, were the first tremors of the great upheaval that was to transform Britain from an agriculturally based economy into an industrially based one. As farming methods improved and the old order of the countryside was thrown awry, traditional crafts and employment on the land fell into decline. These changes at the lower end of the social order had an inevitable and cumulative effect on the rural middle classes whose structure had complemented the old methods of production. It was into this rural bourgeoisie that Thomas Gainsborough was born, and at a critical point in its fortunes.

For centuries Suffolk had been one of the great centres of wool production. Trade in wool had financed the cultural and political adventurism of both the Elizabethans and the Stuarts and had kept the British economy buoyant well into the seventeenth century, since which time it had been in decline. Land was increasingly seen as too precious, given the rapidly expanding population, to be given over to grazing rather than to arable farming. In 1660, in one of the earliest attempts to artificially protect the declining trade, a law was passed decreeing that all shrouds were to be made of wool. Despite this, Gainsborough's father, who had a monopoly of shroud-making in Sudbury – but an unbusinesslike disposition – was bankrupted when Thomas was six years old. This does not seem to have been a catastrophic blow; the Gainsboroughs went on living in the same house, and little or no social disgrace seems then to have been attached to bankruptcy. Doubtless people in such a tightly knit community were more sympathetic than scandalized. John Gainsborough went on to become a burgess of the town, and eventually its postmaster, restoring a degree of financial stability. Thomas's brother Jack and his cousin Samuel were also public figures, being appointed Commissioners of the Stour Navigation, and acting as arbitrators in trade disputes over the use of the river and its amenities (Golding Constable, the painter's father, was also appointed). And so the Gainsboroughs retained their modestly respectable status. But the change of emphasis, from being intimately bound up with the agricultural life of the region to being administrators and civil servants, was a significant one, and typical of the age. Much has been made of Gainsborough's rural upbringing in an attempt to rationalize his devotion to landscape painting, but while it is clear that he retained a strong affection for his home town, for the Suffolk countryside and for countryside in general, he did not really have the clay on his boots which some have claimed. His affiliation was with the middle class, with teachers, clerks, administrators and tradesmen, not with farmers or with what was still often referred to as the 'peasantry'. This is of some significance in assessing both Gainsborough's career and his imagery.

One of the few undisputed facts about Gainsborough's boyhood is that from a very early age drawing was his chief passion. In this he was possibly encouraged by his mother, who is herself thought to

Study of a Sheep, c.1757–9.
Black and white chalks on grey paper, 14.1 × 18.4 cm
Staatliche Museen zu Berlin

have been an amateur watercolourist. The young Thomas spent many hours sketching from nature in the countryside, and seems to have had some informal lessons from a family friend who accompanied him on his walks. Gainsborough retained the habit of sketching all his life, and, when he could, returned to Suffolk or made journeys to other parts of the country to get away from the pressures of the studio. It should be stressed at this point, however, that in his mature landscape works Gainsborough did not attempt to represent the English countryside either in a precise, or in a deliberately archaized, nostalgic way. By the time he had outgrown the chief influences of his formative years – seventeenth- and early eighteenth-century Dutch and French landscapes – his paintings had become sophisticated inventions, with only an indirect relationship to 'real' countryside. This aspect of Gainsborough's work has not always been understood, even during his own lifetime.

We must be very wary of regarding Gainsborough's landscape work – and indeed his portraits, in some senses – as representing anything like a historical

Wooded Landscape with Hawking Party
by Meindert Hobbema (with J. Lingelbach), c.1667.
Oil on canvas, 80.3 × 106 cm
Fitzwilliam Museum, Cambridge

reality, for as depictions of the countryside they bear little resemblance to the actuality of his surroundings. Constable's landscape work, on the other hand, had a very different rationale, and was regarded as shockingly realistic, and one has only to compare the two painters to see to what degree Gainsborough idealized his landscapes. Nevertheless, Gainsborough himself was attacked for what some saw as scenes of unseemly vulgarity – an indication of just how contentious an issue the representation of the countryside was at the end of the 1700s. Gainsborough was undoubtedly aware that his clients did not wish to be shown 'real' countryside, and of the reasons why.

Constable, in his own tribute to Gainsborough, wrote of the Suffolk countryside, 'I fancy I see Gainsborough in every hedge and hollow tree.' By this he meant, of course, not Gainsborough's ghost, but that those features of the landscape looked as if they had been taken from a Gainsborough painting. Landscape art has an insidious and powerful influence on the way we actually perceive the countryside – on the way we look at it, what we look at in it, what we ignore in

it, and how we 'compose' what we see. It is still quite easy, for instance, to go to Dedham Vale and find a view which seems straight out of Constable, but to do so we have to ignore a score of others which do not. Our cultural heritage has conditioned us to view the countryside in a certain way. In fact, it is quite difficult for us to see now what Constable meant, particularly if we examine Gainsborough's mature work, in which the hedges and trees have become highly stylized. Doubtless Constable meant what he said; but he could almost as easily have found parts of Suffolk that reminded him of Ruisdael, or Rubens, if these painters had been his models.

In her biography of Gainsborough, Isabelle Worman makes a succinct judgement on the scanty information about Gainsborough's childhood. Leaving aside the question of his penchant for landscape, she wrote:

His embryonic character developed . . . in the enclosing environment of a small town where he knew next to everybody and next to everybody knew him, and in addition to his own immediate family circle there were grandparents, aunts, uncles and cousins, a small tribe . . . providing a secure framework around his childhood. He would not have understood what is meant by a problem of identity. His roots went deep. He knew who he was.

This is amply borne out by the painter's correspondence and by the testimony of his peers. He might occasionally have doubted his own morality, but never his own judgement. It may be that this sense of security more than hedges and trees accounted for Gainsborough's lifelong attachment to pastoral landscape, which he often represented as a locus of familial bliss.

Gainsborough the painter emerged from this rural milieu with the kind of panache with which he was to repeatedly transform his life and art thereafter. One of his earliest paintings, that now known as *Gainsborough's Forest* or *Cornard Wood* (page 53), was begun while he was still at home in Sudbury. 'It is in

A Pool surrounded by Trees
by Jacob van Ruisdael, c.1665–70.
Oil on canvas, 107.5 × 143 cm
National Gallery, London

some respects a little in the schoolboy stile [sic]', he wrote in the last year of his life, 'the picture was actually painted at Sudbury in 1748 – it was begun before I left school – and was the means of my father sending me to London.' With the benefit of forty years' hindsight he could afford to be critical of the picture, but as we know that Gainsborough was sent to London in 1740, at the age of thirteen, we may surmise that it was the sketches and drawings, and perhaps an early version in oils, which convinced his father that Thomas was destined to be an artist.

As the picture is heavily influenced by the works of Johannes Wijnants (c.1625–84), some scholars have argued that it must have been conceived after Gainsborough's return from London, but this is not necessarily so, as Dutch landscapes remained popular in East Anglia up to and beyond Thomas's childhood, and any middle-class boy with an interest in painting would have seen and very probably copied them. There can be little doubt, however, that in terms of technical expertise a date of 1748 seems more likely for what we see today.

Further proof of what seems to have been a prodigious talent is afforded by the fact that upon his arrival in London, Gainsborough not only secured a place in the workshop of a silversmith (whose name is not known), but also managed from then on to support himself entirely by his own efforts. He was proud to recall that after leaving Sudbury he never cost his father a penny. But his was by no means an overnight success; eight years patiently acquiring technical skills were followed by many years of decidedly modest employment as a professional artist.

London, at the time when Gainsborough first saw it, was in artistic terms a decidedly provincial city. Britain had not produced a painter of international repute for decades, and the three most important and influential painters who had worked in Britain during the previous 150 years had all been immigrants: the Dutchmen Peter Paul Rubens (1577–1640) and Anthony Van Dyck (1599–1641) and the less talented Sir Godfrey Kneller (c.1649–1723), who was a German. Since the great days of the court of Charles I, painting in Britain had become largely cut off from developments on the Continent, and had declined into a minor art form mostly concerned with turgid and mechanical portraiture, its purveyors having a social status little higher than cabinet-makers or metalworkers. The majority of professional artists were still very much under the stylistic influence of Kneller, Principal Painter to William and Mary, whose art was largely derived from that of one of his predecessors in that position, Sir Peter Lely (1618–80). In common with accepted workshop practice at this time, Kneller only painted the face or 'mask' of his sitters, and occasionally the hands. The rest of the picture was filled in by his assistants, or by professionals who specialized in drapery, interiors or landscape backgrounds. The result, not surprisingly, often resembled a mask stuck onto a tailor's dummy. Yet public opinion rated Kneller very highly.

Two figures above all wrested British painting from this trough. In 1739 the Edinburgh-born Allan Ram-

Portrait of Captain Thomas Coram
by William Hogarth, 1740.
Oil on canvas, 243.8 × 152.4 cm
From the Thomas Coram Foundation, London

Boucher and Greuze. Ramsay's Italianate art, which introduced a much-needed sense of colour, vigour and showmanship into the stolid London scene, caused a furore in circles accustomed to a meagre diet of boiled-down Dutch influences (Kneller had been a pupil of Bols, who had been taught by Rembrandt), and would have been intensely discussed by Gainsborough and his friends. Ramsay went on to become Principal Painter in the 1760s.

Ramsay's 'frenchified' style, and that of Jean-Baptiste van Loo (1684–1745), a Provençal of Dutch descent also working in the Rococo style in London, found vigorous opposition in the work of William Hogarth (1697–1764) who was to be the other seminal British influence on Gainsborough. Hogarth, like Gainsborough, began his career apprenticed to a metalworker – in his case a goldsmith – and had begun to work independently as an engraver in the 1720s. He studied painting in his spare time and later taught at one of London's earliest art schools, the semi-official St Martin's Lane Academy. Hogarth was a choleric, bombastic man who hated foreigners and in particular the French, although he travelled in France and was familiar with artistic developments there. By 1730 he was making a name for himself with small conversation pieces, and had began to produce modest portraits, often of middle-class family groups. He might have continued in this quietly successful way, had he not come to realize the paucity and provinciality both of current British painting and of the education he had received. Whereas Ramsay's solution – and later Gainsborough's and Reynolds's too – was to revivify the British tradition with elements directly drawn from developments on the Continent, Hogarth branched out in a different direction. In 1740 he provoked a storm of controversy with his portrait of *Captain Thomas Coram*, the benefactor who had endowed the Foundling Hospital. The portrait was unlike anything London had seen before, for it represented the founder, a middle-class man, in a way previously deemed suitable only for members of the aristocracy and ruling classes. Coram is depicted as a

say (1713–84) arrived in London fresh from Italy, where he had studied under the leading Baroque painter Francesco Solimena (1657–1747), then considered in his homeland to be the greatest living artist. Ramsay had also studied the methods of recent French artists, and his work combined something of the grand manner of the Italian tradition with the new elegance and lightness made fashionable by Watteau,

man of power and culture, as if he were a pillar of society, an admiral or a heroic explorer. By employing this heroic language, Hogarth risked bringing down ridicule upon both himself and his sitter, but the gamble paid off, and the work, and thenceforward Hogarth himself, became a great popular success. This shift in public opinion is a clear indication of the changes that British society was undergoing, changes without which the careers of Gainsborough and Reynolds, to say nothing of those of Ramsay and Lawrence, would have been very different. It marks the rise of the middle class.

Hogarth also realized that one of the key reasons for Britain's artistic provinciality was that there was no public access to new works of art. Until the 1740s London had never seen a public art exhibition, with the exception of displays in auction houses, but these were chiefly of old master paintings. Professional painters worked almost entirely to commission, and paintings went straight from studio to client. An artist might allow visitors to the studio to look over and perhaps buy whatever work had been produced in between commissions, but this was still a very limited audience. In an effort to remedy the situation Hogarth and Coram decided to use the grand buildings of the Foundling Hospital as a showcase for living artists to display their work; Hogarth persuaded many of the leading painters in London to contribute. The exhibition was a great success, and paved the way for annual public exhibitions. Hogarth was also aware that the lack of any formal education for artists in official art schools was another damning indictment of British attitudes towards the status of the artist in society. In the wake of the Foundling Hospital's opening, this situation gradually began to change as a number of artists' societies, clubs and exhibiting societies grew up. This led eventually to the foundation of the Society of Artists, and in the 1760s to the foundation of the Royal Academy of Arts, both of which held annual public exhibitions.

One of Hogarth's friends, and a contributor to Coram's new institution, was Francis Hayman (1708–76). Hayman also taught at the St Martin's Lane Academy, where his pupils included Thomas Gainsborough, and it was probably he who secured a commission for Gainsborough from the hospital in 1748, just before his return to Sudbury. It is a modest, not more than competent, little view of the Charterhouse, painted in a cautious style imitative of Dutch townscape painters such as Pieter de Hooch.

Hayman, known for his rather stiff portraits, was a less important stylistic influence on the young Gainsborough than his colleague at St Martin's Lane, the French painter and engraver Hubert Gravelot (1699–1773). Gravelot, who had been a pupil of Boucher, was together with van Loo chiefly responsible for the dissemination of the Rococo style in London. Few paintings by him survive, and Gainsborough's earliest work in oils shows – with one key exception – almost no French influence, although he undoubtedly did take instruction in painting, as his technical proficiency demonstrates. At this stage Gainsborough seems to have been concentrating, prudently enough, on honing his skills as an engraver so as to be sure of regular if mediocre employment. However, from Gravelot he learned one habit which he was never to abandon and which was to have an overriding influence on his entire œuvre. In order to practise figure composition, Gravelot used simple wooden dolls with jointed limbs. Adapting this practice, Gainsborough later designed and had made his own more sophisticated versions, and his portraits long retained the stiffness of posture and slenderness of limb that resulted from painting from models and not the human form. More significantly, Gainsborough adapted this method to the composition of landscapes, using pieces of twig, rock, coal and even sprouts of broccoli to construct miniature table-top scenes. The implications of this approach for the subsequent development of his landscape art were profound.

We do not know exactly when or where in London Gainsborough first set himself up as a professional painter. Very few paintings survive from before 1750, and most of these seem to have been done in Suffolk either on visits from the capital or after his return to Sudbury. Nor are there any engravings firmly attributable to him – though he is thought to have produced some Rococo designs to frame book illustrations. We can, however, surmise that his chief source of income in the period between leaving the silversmith's workshop – which he probably did after only a few months – and leaving London in 1748, would largely have been from drawings and engravings after other painters' work and from the repair and restoration of oil paintings for dealers and auctioneers. It has even been suggested that he may have forged some Dutch landscapes – he was by 1745 quite able to do so. We know from a surviving sale catalogue that he added some figures to a painting by Wijnants, a common practice to bring new life to an old work or to increase its value. Many years later the sculptor Joseph Nollekens recorded in his diary a remark made by the London silversmith Panton Betew: 'There goes your great Mr Gainsborough. I have many a time had a drawing of his in my shop window before he went to Bath; ay, and he has often been glad to receive seven or eight shillings from me for what I have sold.' This would suggest that Betew was regularly selling Gainsborough's drawings and that perhaps the sum of 'seven or eight shillings' was the remuneration for the sale of more than one drawing. It also implies that Gainsborough continued to send work down to London after leaving the city.

The other certainty about Gainsborough's formal art education is that in common with every other aspiring painter, his chief place of learning would not have been the academy but dealers' rooms and auction houses, where artists would meet daily to discuss and to copy whichever interesting paintings happened to be on show. This again was a habit Gainsborough never lost, and even at the height of his success he was to be seen in the salerooms at Christie's or Phillips studying, copying and, during the sales themselves, making humorous or wry comments about the lots.

When he had the chance, he would visit some of the great private collections, copying works by, among others, Van Dyck, Rubens and Murillo.

So for several years the young Gainsborough found himself in London faced with the not inconsiderable task of earning a living solely by his own hands. His chief source of income was probably reproductive engraving, which was the only affordable means by which the middle classes could enjoy art in their homes. To satisfy what was a growing demand, enormous numbers of engravings of portraits, religious works, conversation pieces and topographical landscapes were being run off and sold for a few pence each. If what we know of the mature Gainsborough is anything to go by, the artist would also have spent a great deal of his time in convivial conversation, drinking and general merry-making. He would also have spent long periods doing nothing in particular; several accounts and his own letters show him turning his back on important commissions for weeks at a time, to the consternation and annoyance of his patrons. Sometimes this was simply because he needed a rest. He was capable of and frequently indulged in astonishing stints of uninterrupted work, as for example when he and his nephew Gainsborough Dupont painted the whole dress in Queen Charlotte's massive portrait in a single night. It is thought that even as a young man he may have been troubled by these fits of melancholy – what we would today describe as clinical depression. This may have been the result of stress and poverty, but there are other possibilities; he may have inherited some tendency to instability from one or other of his parents or, more likely, he was affected by disease. There is strong reason to suppose that he had syphilis, but whether this was contracted before or after his marriage is not known. The disease was rife among certain sectors of the population, and frequently led to mental incapacity and madness.

Throughout his sojourn in London, Gainsborough made periodic visits to Sudbury. On one of these trips

Antoine de la Roque, n.d.
Engraving after Watteau.
Reproduced by courtesy of the Trustees of the British
Museum

---

he met a young woman called Margaret Burr who, according to Gainsborough's earliest biographer, was the sister of a travelling salesman employed by John Gainsborough. The illegitimate daughter of Henry, Duke of Beaufort, she was both beautiful and comparatively wealthy (her father had given her an annuity of £200 though they seem to have been estranged) but, tragically, had inherited syphilis from her father. Despite objections from his parents, Gainsborough and Margaret were married on 15 July 1746 at Dr Keith's Mayfair Chapel, a rather louche establishment that provided a quick, no-questions-asked service. Though his parents did not attend – they may have disapproved of Margaret's illegitimacy, or the social awkwardness of her father being in John's employ – their objections do not seem to have lasted long, and the couple soon moved back to Sudbury into a house only a stone's throw from the family home.

The reasons for this move are not clear. Perhaps Gainsborough felt that he had a better chance of financial security, if not fame and fortune, amongst the farmers and landowners of Suffolk; his father,

who died shortly afterwards, may already have been ill. It is also possible that Margaret, whose tendency to thrift later became an all-consuming obsession, may have been the prime mover. Even so, the decision must have seemed a somewhat retrogressive step to a man already used to supporting himself and on good terms with the likes of Hayman, Hogarth and Gravelot, and apparently poised for better things.

There is reason to suppose that shortly before his removal to Sudbury, Gainsborough had, through the good offices of Hayman, been involved in the decorations for one of the pavilions in the new Vauxhall Gardens; Sir Ellis Waterhouse has identified one of the landscapes as very probably by his hand. The Gardens were the haunt of fashionable London, and for a young man of talent and ambition to suddenly leave the capital after such an important commission seems almost perverse. It was to be a decade before Gainsborough was once again back at the heart of the British art world.

Although there are a considerable number of works dating from the period of Gainsborough's return to Suffolk, they do not enable us to make any firm conclusions about his level of technical expertise or his stylistic intent. They are surprisingly variable, both in quality and in ambition, and reveal, if anything, a restless intelligence searching and experimenting rather than someone who has come to firm conclusions about his art. Nor do we have much more information about his personal circumstances than we do of his first London period.

The five or six earliest surviving pictures are clearly strongly indebted to the Dutch landscape tradition – an influence so pervasive that Gainsborough seems sometimes to have settled for a somewhat clumsy composition because it looks more Dutch, rather that adopting the more radical and satisfactory solutions of which he was undoubtedly capable. On the other hand, certain aspects of his technique – the ability to use light as a unifying factor, for example – reveal a precocious talent at odds with his sometimes naïve rendition, in particular, of the human figure.

The most famous of these early works is probably the double portrait of *Mr and Mrs Andrews*, painted in Sudbury around 1748 and now in the National Gallery, London (page 55). There are several curious and telling features to this work, which was commissioned as a marriage portrait by Andrews, a wealthy yeoman from Bulmer, a village a few miles from Sudbury. Very probably the Andrews were old friends of the family. We do not know whether the couple gave specific instructions to the painter, except that Mrs Andrews expressed a wish to be shown with a pheasant in her lap, but whatever their intentions, the portrait they eventually received was far from conventional in its approach.

Gainsborough's interest in the landscape element of the composition – and possibly his lack of confidence with the human form – has here led him to place the couple at the extreme margin of the work. As a result

A Gypsy Scene, *c.1746–7.*
Oil on canvas, 31.4 × 36.8 cm
Cincinnati Art Museum, Ohio

of this unusual format, the composition is almost two pictures, portrait and landscape, side by side. It is clearly unfinished, particularly the detail on Mrs Andrews's dress, and her lap has been scraped almost clean of paint. But it is the curiously doll-like execution of the figures that first holds the attention. The use of dolls as compositional models was commonplace – though not universal – and the sitters would not have expected to visit the studio for longer than it took to paint their faces. In fact, Mrs Andrews's pose and dress is lifted entirely from Gainsborough's own marriage portrait. Despite this static quality, however, as portraits they are perfectly convincing, full of character, and clearly rendered, if without finesse. Gainsborough has closely matched the facial features but has not managed to unify them convincingly with the heads; as one of his friends remarked on seeing his portraits for the first time, they are 'perfectly like, but stiffly drawn'. This awkwardness is noticeably at odds with the superb and confidently rendered landscape beyond, filled with the detail that Gainsborough loved to add, such as the gate, the flock of sheep, and the church tower to the extreme left.

There are several other interesting features. Mr Andrews's right foot seems inordinately large; his wife's dress, crisp and quite brilliantly executed on the left-hand side, is apparently unfinished on the right and does not lie convincingly against the seat (a seat which is surely a little Rococo invention by Gainsborough). The area between the figures and the edge of the cornfield is curiously flat and blurred, suggesting that something has been painted over or left out – perhaps another dog or an earlier version of the animal squashed rather clumsily between Mr Andrews and the left-hand edge, but more probably the crisply painted plants usually found in the foreground of Dutch-style landscapes. Yet against these anomalies must be pointed out the exceptionally fine execution of the oak tree, the marvellously adroit play of light over Mr Andrews's coat, and the challenging, artifically extended perspective. The portrait is a small work – surprisingly small – but its conception is bold and implies a much greater pictorial ambition. Despite its curious uneasiness there is no denying its success, though perhaps if it had been seen in London at the time it would have been strongly criticized, even ridiculed, for it exhibits few of the rules which taste and fashion dictated for such works. We regard it today as a confident statement of the comfortable inheritance and social standing of its subjects; the land – productive, ordered, well-tended – is theirs. They are at ease in it but not really of it. Mr Andrews's inheritance allows him the luxury of sport rather than the grinding toil of forcing produce from the soil. Those who do work the land are invisible, yet they too are by implication given to Mrs Andrews upon her marriage; the signs of their labour are in the forefront of the picture. This simple coded message of class may today appear vulgarly ostentatious, but at the time Gainsborough was flouting convention by showing the couple anywhere near 'real' farmland. It would have been more acceptable to have shown them in an Arcadian, more formal landscape, which signified their landed status and, by concealing any view of agricultural land, more decorously alluded to their life of leisure.

It is tempting to see the picture as a deliberate attempt to weld together the more realist Dutch landscape tradition with the more genteel English tradition of country portraiture of the kind produced by Devis and Stubbs. In one sense one can almost see the join in the clumsy horizontal which separates foreground from background. On the right of the picture there is no middleground at all. Here the line implies a drop in the land and a sizeable tract of 'dead ground' out of sight. On the left, beyond the tree trunk, Gainsborough has fudged a solution to this problem by raising the horizon above the trees, which have thus become the middle rather than the background. Once this is perceived, the weakness of the construction is difficult to ignore but, as with the stiff figures, it matters little, for the picture's naivety and unconventional composition are a vital part of its appeal. It should be said, too, that in comparison with similar

works in the genre in Britain at the time – again Devis and Stubbs come to mind – the picture is both bold and fluent. In this work, one of the greatest of all eighteenth-century British portraits, Gainsborough sets out boldly, if a little clumsily, the concerns that he was to explore throughout his life. The tension between the problems of landscape and portrait painting, which was to become a dominant feature of his career, is here exemplified at the very beginning of his professional life; that he should have attempted to shackle the two genres together in such a direct way and so early on is perhaps an indication of his uncomplicated and clear-sighted nature.

The portrait of Mr and Mrs Andrews represents the first sign of Gainsborough's promise as an innovative artist, but there are indications in three earlier pictures of his youthful experimentation. The first of these is *Crossing the Ford* (page 45), a landscape dated to *c*.1754–5, when Gainsborough was about eighteen years old. This tiny picture, though lacking any spark of originality, is an astonishingly able pastiche which, as Waterhouse remarked, might almost pass for the work of Wijnants. It is by no means well-structured compositionally, though the works which it slavishly imitates often display similar clumsiness. The tree is not particularly convincing; its branches mirror too closely the pattern of the clouds and are somewhat two-dimensional. The bank on which it sits is awkward and the relative sizes of the animals and figure in relation to the middle distance are questionable. The cottage seems to be tilted and the bridge too distant for its place in the perspective. But once more there are elements – particularly the use of lighting and some of the detailed rendition of the animals – which though conventional are executed with great facility. The format, with the high, pale bank in the left foreground, was one to which Gainsborough returned again and again over the years, adding and subtracting various elements.

Some twelve months later, in the *A View in Suffolk* (page 49), now in Dublin, we can see the astonishing pace with which Gainsborough has assimilated influences and begun to develop a personal approach to this kind of landscape. There is no denying that this work is laid out in the Dutch manner, with its deep, rapidly receding perspective, low horizon and overtly ornamental cloudscape. In execution, however, it is entirely different. Though not much larger than *Crossing the Ford*, it is filled with exuberance and stuffed with detail, from the ruts in the cart track to the strata of the rocks, from the sunlit treetrunks to the delicate foreground plants. The complexity of the land surface is exaggerated by the patchy light, and although there are indistinct passages – such as the chalk rubble in the left foreground – these are counterbalanced by such bravura touches as the white donkey silhouetted on the cliff top against the dark cloud. In conception the work is Dutch; in execution it owes much to French painting; and the highly animated surface puts it firmly in the Baroque tradition. But the result is entirely Gainsborough's own; the trees, for example, are not the flimsy confections of Fragonard or Watteau, but are solidly realistic. The balance, or rather deliberate imbalance, of land and cloud masses is a considerable improvement on his earlier work. Although the light is complex and the overall colour scheme rather pallid, there is none of the insubstantiality characteristic of French landscape; there is a solid three-dimensionality and the perspective makes perfect sense, with no fudging or trickery.

Gainsborough was as familiar with French art as with Dutch, as is evidenced by the third of the early paintings, of a couple seated on a bench (page 51), widely supposed to be a self-portrait with his fiancée Margaret (although the setting implies courtship, it may have been painted after their marriage). Despite being probably painted in the same year as the Dublin landscape, one might suppose it was by a completely different hand. Gainsborough has chosen a deliberately, almost exaggerately French Rococo style for the subject – perhaps to show off his skill as a pasticheur. The trees have a feathery, schematic quality derived directly from Watteau and his followers, a technique

that Gainsborough was later to adapt to his own ends. The Arcadian setting, complete with rotunda, is ultimately derived from the classicized landscapes of Claude Lorrain and Poussin filtered through French Rococo art. Again, the handling of the dress is exceptionally delicate, though in a more hard-edged manner than Watteau or Fragonard would have attempted, and the surface detail of the dress shows that that of Mrs Andrews is indeed unfinished. Although Margaret has a stiff, doll-like posture and face, Gainsborough's own features are quite recognizable, particularly his long, pointed nose. He gestures toward his fiancée, inviting us to admire his good fortune, whilst putting down a book; he no longer needs to read romances, he has his own.

Landscape with a Goatherd and Goats
by Claude Lorrain, c.1636.
Oil on canvas, 51.4 × 41.3 cm
National Gallery, London

Few other paintings definitely datable to the three or four years in Sudbury survive. There is a view of St Mary's Church, Hadleigh, now housed in the Gainsborough's House museum at Sudbury; a small portrait of the artist, his wife and their first daughter Mary; and the early landscape masterpiece *Cornard Wood* (page 53). This work, finished in 1748 but perhaps begun many years earlier, is by far the most famous of Gainsborough's early landscapes, and one of his best-known pictures. Again, the Dutch influence is clearly visible, and there is little sign of the Rococo ornateness of the *View in Suffolk* of a few years earlier, which implies that *Cornard Wood* was indeed conceived and laid out some years previously. It bears comparison with the landscape work of Rubens, which he deeply admired and later collected. Early in his career Gainsborough painted, sometimes to commission, several topographical views, which were at the time the only type of landscape work which would find a ready market. More fanciful landscape scenes were occasionally commissioned for the interiors of grand houses – usually in pairs to hang either side of a fireplace – hence the term 'chimneypieces'. But these were regarded as mere decorations rather than significant works of art; they tended to be formulaic, sentimental scenes of courting milkmaids and swains, often in a vaguely classical setting. *Cornard Wood* must, however, have been a labour of love, and merges the Dutch tradition with the English topographical one. Few of the weaknesses apparent in *Crossing the Ford* are repeated here.

One of the most curious things about it is that the figures are so well realized in comparison to those in his portraits. The posture and limbs of the boy leaning on a spade, and the woodcutter roping together faggots – both possibly derived from Dutch originals – are completely convincing. The picture is full of intricate, brilliant detail, and the handling of the shafting light is masterful, particularly in the warm foreground patch and on the upper bank in the left middle distance. The shadows, where the difficulty is to retain three-dimensionality, also work well, with receding pools on the right balancing the track, and there are fine small touches too, such as the twisted gorse bush above the sleeping dog. The one inconsistency is the scale of the oak tree in the foreground, which is perhaps too small for a mature tree in that position given the height of the walking figure on the track behind and that of the woodcutter in the foreground. It is, despite this, a daring and accomplished work, using a clever distortion of perspective to open up the track and the pools away from the viewer. Although it would have seemed somewhat outré to English eyes at the time, particularly those used to the work of the contemporary French landscapists, the picture changed hands several times during Gainsborough's lifetime and came to be recognized as his most accomplished early works, even if the artist himself considered it 'a little in the schoolboy stile'. It marks, perhaps, the first step in an English landscape tradition that was to come to full fruition in the work of John Constable.

So it would seem that on his marriage and return to Sudbury, Gainsborough was still flexing his artistic muscles, restlessly mixing the styles by which he had been influenced, but above all able to pick and choose elements from them at will. It is clear that he had spent a great deal of time working on his landscape technique, but he soon came to realize that if he was to make a living as a painter, it was on portraiture that he would have to concentrate. In 1748 his father died, and it may have been this event which persuaded Gainsborough to settle permanently in Suffolk. This year also marked the birth of his first child Mary, which may have focused his attention with renewed vigour on the serious issue of making a living.

At first the Gainsboroughs found it difficult to keep the wolf from the door, and Thomas turned his hand to any kind of painting work which came his way, even sign-painting. In 1752 his second daughter Margaret was born and it became clear that Sudbury, for all its familiarity, could never provide the volume of work the family required to make a living. They moved to the much larger town of Ipswich, a major market town of some 10,000 inhabitants, with a thriving port. Gainsborough lost no time in immersing himself in the social life of the town which was far more cosmopolitan and cultured than Sudbury. Foremost in his activities was the Music Society. Gainsborough was a passionate amateur musician and played several instruments including the harpsichord, violin and viol da Gamba – though opinions varied as to his capabilities. His friend the musician William Jackson thought that he had a natural ear but little application; as with intellectual conversation Gainsborough seems to have passed muster by clever improvization. He quickly became an indispensable and dedicated member of the group, and although he seems not to have produced the group portrait or conversation piece we might have expected, a number of sketches of musicians survive.

The move to Ipswich proved to be a sensible one. Although there is evidence that Gainsborough was from time to time in debt and in arrears with his rent, generally speaking he kept his head above water, and found a fairly constant demand for his services as a portraitist among the middle and upper classes of the area. Occasionally a more prestigious commission came his way, such as the portrait of Admiral Vernon of 1753, now in the National Portrait Gallery, London. By 1757 he was actually finding it difficult to keep up with the demand for his work, as we learn from a letter to a gentleman in Colchester (twenty miles away) in which Gainsborough apologizes for not coming to visit as promised because he is loath to turn away custom in Ipswich.

During these years most of Gainsborough's portraits are painted to an unvarying formula, using a *trompe l'œil* oval surround and a half-length or head-and-shoulders pose against a plain dark background. He turned out scores of such pictures, and they are variable in quality. Some of them do, however, reveal interesting minor variations and technical experimentation. Others are sketchily done, obviously in haste, and it is noticeable that the finest of them are those of family friends or friends of friends. All, one would suppose, bear a resemblance to the sitter, but these few are imbued with something more. Among the best of them are the portraits of the *Reverend Richard Canning* and of *Mrs John Kirby* (see pages 71 and 67). Canning's in particular is superb, the face when viewed at the appropriate distance resembling the hyper-real portrait work of Dürer. When the figures are set in the open air, they retain their doll-like stiffness, as with the uncomfortably-placed but apparently benign Mr Plampin and the doe-eyed Lloyd children (pages 59 and 57).

In his later years, in common with most of his rivals, Gainsborough expressed his boredom with and distate for 'phiz-mongery' – tedious churning out of formula portraits to make a living. He is said to have been the first to use the term 'pot-boiler' to describe such workaday pieces; on being asked why he persisted with portraiture when his first love was landscape, he replied, 'to keep the pot boiling' (other sources say that his rival John Hoppner coined the phrase). However, there can be no doubt that this constant stream of mundane portraits was essential not only to his physical wellbeing but also to his development of technical expertise. Gradually, by endless repetition, he acquired the knack not just of achieving a likeness, but of breathing life into his 'phizzes'. It was the best possible training, and it is probably no bad thing that the steady demand for portraits kept him from concentrating exclusively on his landscape work, for there can be little doubt that given half a chance, that is what he would have done, despite the financial disincentive.

By this time – the mid-1750s – Gainsborough's working practices were firmly established. He persisted with the use of dolls to compose group portraits, but it was his *method* of portrait painting which caused most comment. He developed a technique of painting in half-light, with curtains drawn and candles lit, and with the sitter placed not before him but at a right angle to the canvas. Using brushes tied to long handles he would paint from a spot located at exactly the same distance from the picture as from the subject. By this means he was able to concentrate from the outset on achieving a likeness which would have its optimum effect at the distance from which it would be viewed when hung. The fine detail and the colouring were overlaid at a later stage, presumably in daylight. The result of this – apart from portraits so lifelike that they astonished his contemporaries – was that the colour and brushwork of his completed pictures became increasingly personal, divorced as they were from the early stages of each work. Gainsborough tended, for example, to use a strong reddish-purple tinge in his flesh tones, which some thought gave his sitters too high a colour (the current fashion for women was an almost death-like pallor). In the overworking of the preliminary likeness the brushwork became an integral part of the composition rather than following the dictates of the sitter's physiognomy. As a result, Gainsborough achieved a mastery of brushwork to which none of his contemporaries came close.

For Gainsborough the painting, not the subject, was important. This determination to make a picture rather than just a likeness is crucial to understanding Gainsborough's work, for it was his main consideration in both landscapes and portraits. For him the picture was everything, things outside being secondary to the logic and reality of the work itself. This seems a surprisingly modern attitude to art, but should not be confused with the kind of theorizing about painting which arose during the twentieth century. Gainsborough was not interested either in an art which slavishly copied reality, or in one in which painting developed only with reference to itself. Instead, he sought to produce works which, though having as their subject matter real people and real objects, represented them in a language that unified them in a new reality. To him, art was something entirely separate from the things it depicted and entirely different to the world which gave birth to it.

In many respects this explains why Gainsborough came to rely exclusively on composing model landscapes from which to paint his later masterpieces. We find him in the 1760s writing to Lord Hardwicke, who had requested a topographical landscape:

If his Lordship wishes to have anything tollerable of the name of G. the Subject altogether, as well as figures &c must be of his own Brain; otherwise Lord Hardwicke will only pay for Encouraging a Man out of his Way – and had much better buy a Picture of some of the good Old Masters.

The message is clear: Gainsborough was not interested in portraying actual scenes, but in creating them. His landscapes were highly personal and poetic, and he felt that they should be judged not as wonders of nature, but as products of the artist's intellect and skill – an attitude which indicates a determination on the part of the artist to raise the status of painting to that then enjoyed by literature and poetry. Similarly, it was the beauties of the portrait rather than those of the sitter that he felt ought to be the first object of public interest. This was an attitude unfortunately not understood or shared by very many of his contemporaries, and Gainsborough's insistence upon it later led him into a series of vitriolic disputes over what he felt was the lack of respect given to his instructions for the hanging of his pictures. Another consequence of this outlook was that unlike most of his rivals, Gainsborough rarely employed a 'drapery man'. He only ever had one assistant, his nephew Gainsborough Dupont, and was renowned – and sometimes ridiculed – for concerning himself with every stage and aspect of the picture. Even Dupont is thought to have been more of an apprentice than an assistant, though he certainly collaborated on a number of works, particularly when the master was behind schedule, which was often. But Gainsborough maintained that no part of any picture was more or less important than any other, and prided himself on his meticulousness. He was also, of course, the best drapery man there was, and he knew it.

During the Ipswich years it was the steady volume of work, rather than any great financial successes, which kept Gainsborough afloat. At this time he was charging five guineas for a portrait head, this rising to eight guineas in about 1757. Half-lengths cost fifteen guineas, and the rare full-lengths probably twenty-five or thirty guineas. For small landscapes he charged fifteen or twenty guineas. The leading young painters in London at the time, Hudson and Reynolds, were then charging up to fifteen guineas for a head and thirty for a half-length; but there were signs that Gainsborough's reputation – and with it his financial worth – was growing. By the late 1750s he frequently travelled away from home, moving from one country seat to another producing both portraits and landscapes for their wealthy inhabitants. In 1758 he toured Buckinghamshire and Oxfordshire in this way.

Within his social circle at Ipswich were several friends who were to prove of lasting help to Gainsborough. Among them was Joshua Kirby, a devout and principled man who became (perhaps surprisingly, given Gainsborough's hedonistic outlook) a lifelong friend and one of his most ardent promoters. Kirby, who became Clerk of Works at Kew Palace and was on familiar terms with King George III, secured Gainsborough his first London commission (for two landscapes) from the Duke of Bedford.

Samuel Kilderbee and his wife were enthusiastic finders of clients for Gainsborough during the Ipswich years, and sat for him themselves. Kilderbee, later Town Clerk of Ipswich, was a bright, successful young lawyer, and exactly the sort of well-connected, ambitious person that Gainsborough needed to cultivate. William Wollaston, a keen amateur flautist whom Gainsborough probably met at the Music Society, became MP for Ipswich and was the subject of the artist's earliest-known standing full-length portrait. The most significant meeting, however, was with Philip Thicknesse. This singularly strange, egotistical, unstable and possibly unscrupulous man was then the governor of Landguard Fort, situated a few

miles down river opposite the strategically important harbour at Harwich. He was Gainsborough's first posthumous biographer, although they were estranged for the latter part of the painter's life. He relates how they met when Thicknesse was fooled by a small painting Gainsborough had propped up on his garden wall, into thinking he was looking at a real person. The picture, known as *Tom Peartree* and now in the Christchurch Mansion Museum, Ipswich, shows a young man whom Gainsborough had seen leaning over the wall gazing avidly at the ripe pears on his tree. He subsequently placed the painting on top of the wall as a kind of advertisement, and Thicknesse, impressed, knocked at his door and introduced himself. It was to prove a turning point in Gainsborough's career.

Thicknesse may not have been a particularly likeable man but he undoubtedly had an eye for talent. He was shown into the studio and saw there, amongst other things, the portrait of Admiral Vernon, whom he knew. Surprisingly, given contemporary taste, he realized immediately that Gainsborough's landscape work was of a far higher quality than his portraiture – it was he who remarked that Gainsborough's portraits were 'perfectly like but stiffly drawn'. He promptly commissioned two landscapes for his quarters at Landguard Fort, one of the few topographical commissions that Gainsborough ever accepted, of the coast nearby (unfortunately destroyed later by damp, though an engraving of one survives). Thicknesse became for a time Gainsborough's closest friend and most tireless promoter, despite the immediate dislike taken to him by the artist's wife.

In the paintings of the Ipswich period (*c*.1750–9) we are again confronted by some curious technical and stylistic anomalies as Gainsborough continued his uneven progression towards competence in portraiture: 'I am the most inconsistent changeable being, so full of fitts and starts', he wrote. In the stiffness and formality of *Heneage Lloyd and his Sister* and *John Plampin* (pages 57 and 59), there is little to prefigure the startlingly vivid and well-modelled picture of his daughters chasing a butterfly of *c.*1755–6 (page 69). Though this work is unfinished, it is quite clear that Gainsborough's technical expertise has developed apace: the arms and legs have lost their thin doll-like quality, the faces are fully unified with the heads and, above all, there is a strong sense of movement and dynamism in the composition. Although the first impression is that the two children are moving from right to left across the canvas, closer examination shows that the older girl is walking forwards rather than across, and the younger turning away after the insect. This effect would have been more striking had Gainsborough finished the lower right-hand side of the picture, giving the impression that they are about to pass one on either side of the viewer. The dappled highlights on the younger girl's dress suggests that she is further back, heightening the impression of forward motion. Gainsborough's facility with drapery is once again apparent, but the picture has none of the individualistic brushwork which typifies his later pictures; it seems rather to mark a transitional phase. As it was obviously done for his own satisfaction rather than as a commission, we may suppose that Gainsborough left it unfinished because of the press-ure of other work; he remarked at the time that he owed only six pounds, although some time later we find him borrowing heavily again. Possibly, however, he simply grew bored of it. In another unfinished picture of his daughters, painted in 1758 (page 75), the children have already taken on the rather sombre, self-absorbed look characteristic of all his later por-traits of them. But here his approach to the composi-tion seems to have been radically different, with a far more vigorous and rhythmic handling of the paint. In the portrait of *The Reverend Canning* (page 71) another experiment is visible: an intricate system of crosshatching to model the features. It is clear from Gainsborough's later letters that he wanted his brush-work not just to be visible to, but also appreciated by any viewer situated at the conventional distance from the work; he wanted to show not just what he had done, but how he had done it, and how well.

Portrait of Henrietta Vernon, Lady Grosvenor, wife of Richard, 1st Earl Grosvenor, *c.*1766–7.
Oil on canvas, 76.2 × 63.5 cm
With kind permission of His Grace
The Duke of Westminster

Thus we may conclude that he envisaged himself not simply as an artist in the poetic sense, an inventor of scenes and manipulator of emotions, but also as a master craftsman. Many artists have consciously chosen to pursue just one of these ideals; Gains-borough wanted to be both. Yet he was still capable of what now seem to us the most extraordinary lapses. A number of full-length portraits dating from the late Ipswich and early Bath period display the same stiffness and timidity that marked his first essays in the genre. This may in part have been due to his self-confessed 'fits and starts', his periodic lapses into melancholia or at the least into a profound ennui. The least satisfactory pictures may indicate those sitters with whom he felt the least empathy or who could spare him the least time – he never altered a face without the sitter being present, so on occasion must have been left with a picture which the client regarded as finished but which he felt had not been properly concluded. His correspondence is full of letters to anxious and sometimes angry clients demanding their portraits, to which he responds either with apologies or with unconcealed irritation. On occasion, portraits were still not finished two years after the initial sitting, though when the mood took him Gainsborough was a speedy worker, capable of completing the largest commissions in two weeks. Once again his best work seems to be of women, though his interest was not always entirely professional.

Even at the height of his career during the 1770s and 1780s we can still detect those pictures on which he exercised special care. We are used, when examining the mature œuvre of artists, to seeing all the works brought to the same level of finish and displaying consistent, if still developing style. In these respects Gainsborough's work is far less uniform than that of many artists, and if we compare it to that of Constable, for example, whose only significant mature change came very late in his career, it seems indeed a thing of fits and starts. It should be remembered, however, that in Gainsborough's case the circumstances of production, particularly after 1760 when demands on his time were many, mitigated against his being able to apply himself equally to each commission, even supposing he had had the inclination.

We have already discussed Gainsborough's earliest landscape work and noted that Philip Thicknesse, for one, perceived its high standard. This is surprising because, as John Hayes, the leading authority on Gainsborough's landscapes, has remarked, the early landscapes were 'totally with precedent in English painting'. One would suppose, then, that to a man such as Thicknesse and to most contemporary observers they would seem not merely unusual but even bizarre. Gainsborough was not simply ignoring the established topographical and 'chimney-piece' traditions, but displaying a radically new creative impulse, which sought to combine the language of Dutch landscape painting – peopled by peasants and animals and with an evident close relationship to contemporary reality – with a classical, Arcadian tradition derived from French and Italian models. The viewer was to feel that he or she was looking at an Arcadian scene, despite the fact that the elements of the composition were not classical but, to use a slightly later term, 'naturalistic', albeit with a distinctly retrospective tinge. The paintings were, Hayes implies, recognizably English rather than Dutch.

John Barrell, in his influential essay on eighteenth-century perceptions of landscape and the development of the pastoral tradition in British culture (a tradition in which we can firmly place Gainsborough's landscapes), has argued that this new iconography should be seen as part of an ideological struggle arising from the rapid disintegration of traditional methods of agricultural work in Britain (a subject touched on earlier), and the consequent changes in class perception. His work is closely founded on that of the historians E.P. Thompson and Raymond Williams. These changes, according to Barrell, gave rise to a widespread cultural debate in which notions of work, recreation, poverty, social harmony and so on were all thrown into question, resulting in new forms of representation of the countryside – in literature, poetry and painting – that were sometimes mutually exclusive or contemporaneous but opposed.

Barrell locates Gainsborough's landscape work at the centre of this cultural debate, arguing that its iconography allows us to identify strong similarities in its message to the work of poets such as Goldsmith and Crabbe. This is doubtless true, though what is far less obvious is Gainsborough's own perception of this process or of his position within it. No one, least of all Barrell, would suggest that Gainsborough was deliberately forging a new tradition in British landscape painting in response to what he perceived to be

Rocky Wooded Landscape with Mounted Drover,
Horses Watering at a Trough and
Distant Village and Mountains, *1780.*
Oil on canvas, 123 × 99 cm
Private Collection

changes in the ideologies of certain social groups. But there can be no doubt that his ability to produce such radical work was in part due to an awareness of other new representations of landscape, particularly in poetry and prose, and to his intimacy with members of the aristocracy and landed gentry and with the countryside itself. Contemporaries stress that he was on familiar terms with people of all social classes, as comfortable with agricultural labourers as with their masters. His increasingly Romantic vision of rural England (if we can wholly accept that an idea of 'England' is what he is portraying) bears comparison with that of Wordsworth, showing as it does labour-

ers and peasants engaged in honest toil in an atmosphere of tranquillity. His vision would have reassured his clients that it was possible to envisage such social harmony whilst stopping short of representing it as actual fact. It could be argued, and Barrell certainly implies it, that these works should be taken as statements of a contemporary ideal rather than as sentimental and nostalgic exercises in fantasy, which would be our logical appraisal of them. They were thus in some senses as much forward-looking as retrospective and as much political – in the loosest sense – as purely decorative. But in such debates so much is conditional upon variable factors such as the context and the reception of such images, rather than the simple circumstances of production or intent, that no unequivocal statement of either the artist's intentions or of his clients' perception of the finished works is possible. It should not be thought, either, that the meaning of these paintings was crystal clear to the audience, or that what they portrayed seemed straightforward or uncontentious, even at the time. Indeed, there is strong evidence that while to some Gainsborough's landscapes seemed strongly Romantic and poetic, to others they appeared coarse and dangerously at odds with accepted taste – perhaps even subversive. Gainsborough's contemporary, John Hoppner (1758–1810), for example, writing in the 1780s when Gainsborough was at the height of his popularity and resident in Pall Mall, London, composed a satirical piece of advice to aspiring artists:

If you paint for the connoisseurs, never attempt at simple elegance, picturesque ideas of nature, brilliancy of colouring or taste in the groupings of your figures. Leave all that to the gentleman in Pall Mall who is so cursedly obstinate that he fills his canvas with unthatched cottages and their bare-legged inhabitants. This is VULGAR NATURE – *pray avoid it.*

It is evident that Gainsborough's work did not receive universal critical approval, although he had his ardent supporters in the press, notably his close friend Henry Bate-Dudley. Hoppner seems to imply that the very artificial, Picturesque nature of Gainsborough's late work was rejected by some arbiters of taste by reason of its content if not also its style. It must be stressed that Gainsborough's letters and the memoirs of his contemporaries leave us in no doubt that he intended his pictures as purely poetic, aesthetic exercises without any didactic role. But this is not to say, of course, that they did not subsequently acquire or fulfil such a role in the ongoing cultural and political debate thrown up by severe social changes.

In 1759 Gainsborough moved to Bath, probably at the suggestion of Philip Thicknesse, who had a house there, and certainly with his financial help. Bath was then coming into its heyday as the most fashionable spa town, a reputation it continued to enjoy until the advent of Continental travel at the beginning of the nineteenth century. Bath was a resort where the rich and famous went to rest after the rigours of London society, and where pillars of the Establishment promenaded alongside the ostentatiously nouveau riche. Gainsborough's neighbours in Bath included William Pitt and Clive of India. The move was a gamble, and was resisted by Margaret, who was terrified of the expense despite their by now modestly comfortable existence. Thicknesse found them a house to rent at fifty guineas a year. When she protested, Thicknesse – who probably hoped to profit by association – retorted that so confident was he of his friend's abilities that if necessary he would take a house at 150 guineas and pay the rent himself. Margaret need not have worried; her husband's only significant rival in the town was the minor, and largely now forgotten portraitist William Hoare. Gainsborough quickly found that demand for his work exceeded his capacity to provide it. He soon raised his prices to twenty guineas a head and forty for a half-length, which were only slightly less than the fees then currently being charged in London by Reynolds, now firmly established as the leading British artist.

It has often been said that Gainsborough's move to Bath corresponds to a revolution in his work as a portraitist; that the formal, often stiff work of the Ipswich years suddenly gives way to a radically new and brilliant style. This is an oversimplification. It would be truer to say that after leaving Ipswich he increasingly experimented with his approach to portraiture, probably because he was addressing a more open-minded, cosmopolitan, even perhaps sensation-seeking public. Within three or four years of his move to Bath a new, bravura manner of painting, personal and highly animated, gradually came to replace the more traditional and cautious style of the Ipswich period. But for a time the styles coexisted. Gainsborough is noticeably more willing to experiment in his portraits of women than in those of men. Much work remains to be done to identify the reasons behind this. There is little doubt that he enjoyed painting women more than men, but it seems that there must also have been a significant change in the public perception of women and their perception of themselves and their aspirations. This is a change which has a strong bearing, for instance, on the rise of the novel and the work of such writers as Jane Austen, who was portraying Bath society slightly later. Women were acquiring a new glamour and social standing, and Gainsborough captures the moment.

The painting which is often said to mark the radical reorientation of Gainsborough's work is the portrait of Ann Ford (page 77), Philip Thicknesse's fiancée, done immediately after the move to Bath. Certainly there is little in the Ipswich work to prepare us for the exuberance of this picture, which displays many of the characteristics of his late portraits of fashionable society ladies: a rich, warm palette, free and dynamic brushwork, a challenging pose and a pyrotechnical display of ornate drapery-work, this last derived from Van Dyck, whom Gainsborough idolized. It would be wrong to claim that henceforth Gainsborough always painted in this manner or that the picture in question was greeted with immediate acclaim. As one observer remarked: 'A most extraordinary painting, handsome and bold; but I should be very sorry to have anyone I loved set forth in such a manner.'

What seems a more likely explanation of this apparently considered and confident shift in his style is that Gainsborough felt able to experiment because of his close friendship with Philip and Ann Thicknesse, who would have known that he was always keen to try out new styles and techniques, and would have encouraged him. We have seen that from a very early stage in his career Gainsborough was able to master radically different styles with equal assurance, as the juxtaposition of the French-influenced double portrait with his wife and any of the early Dutch-influenced works demonstrates. That there is no surviving work closely related to *Mrs Philip Thicknesse* does not necessarily mean that the picture had no precedent, but most scholars have chosen to hail the singularity of the work as evidence of a great stylistic advance despite the conventional, though increasingly assured approach evident in such works as *The Byam Family* and *General Johnston* (pages 85 and 83) painted not long afterwards.

His portrait of *Uvedale Price* of 1760 (page 79), for example is very close to work of the Ipswich years – such as the portrait of the *Reverend Richard Canning*. General Johnston's portrait, though it shows Gainsborough experimenting with the pose of his sitters, is by no means as confident a work as that of the more conventionally posed *John Wilkinson* (page 105), and a very long way from the grandeur and overbearing presence of *John Campbell* (page 91). Comparison between *General Johnston* and Reynolds's relaxed and effortlessly poised *Colonel St Leger* shows just how far Gainsborough still had to go to compete with the best contemporary portraiture. *Mrs Thicknesse*, for all its striking originality, is not entirely satisfactory in terms of the pose – the angle of the body, though partly concealed by the eye-catching antique dress, is odd – and has strong purplish flesh tones, particularly in the face, which must have jarred with conventional notions of beauty. Yet we have only to recall *The Painter's Daughters chasing a Butterfly* (page 69) to satisfy ourselves that Gainsborough was eminently capable of portraying

movement, well rounded limbs and convincing torsoes. Why then the stick-limbed General Johnston? The answer must lie in his continuing reliance on dolls or dummies for the pose of the majority of his sitters. It is not until the late 1760s that we can confidently identify a complete and permanent revision of his portrait technique.

Colonel John Hayes St Leger
by Sir Joshua Reynolds, 1778.
Oil on canvas, 240 × 147.3 cm
The National Trust, Waddesdon Manor

It seems likely that one of the strongest influences on Gainsborough's willingness to experiment with portraiture was his landscape work. His new-found financial security and his rapid rise to fame (within three years of the move he was seriously ill due to overwork, probably exacerbated by venereal disease) afforded him much greater opportunity to work on his landscapes than would have been possible in Suffolk. In the landscapes of the early 1760s we can see that he is working at a type of scene in which the traditional pastoral elements – milkmaids, drovers, cattle and woodmen – are displayed in a topography which, although comprised of naturalistic elements, is composed in such a way as to make it immediately obvious to the viewer that it is intended to be appreciated as a formal arrangement not just within the two dimensions of the framed surface but within the third dimension of the suggested depth 'beyond'. Thus, while it is obvious that a work such as the *Grand Landscape* at Worcester, Massachussetts (page 81) is greatly indebted to the work of Rubens (see *The Watering Place*), it exemplifies just how far Gainsborough has moved on from the simple formal arrangement of his work of the late 1740s and early 1750s. The Worcester landscape – which marks Gainsborough's maturity as a landscape artist – is a wholly Baroque composition, and hugely ambitious in its use of perspective. It is constructed in a spiral like the interior of a shell, with three separate 'chambers' leading the eye gradually back via the flock of sheep and the horse to the dead, sunlit tree trunk at the second level, to the brightly lit woodland in the 'inner' chamber accented by the two cattle placed in front. There is no real 'background' here, in the simple sense of the background of *Mr and Mrs Andrews* or of the glimpsed horizon in *Cornard Wood* (pages 55 and 53). All parts of the picture are equally important, and depth has become an integral part of the subject rather than merely incidental to it. The paint is handled with greater freedom and energy, and the palette is significantly more bold than in previous work. Although this *Grand Landscape* could never for a moment be mistaken for a record of a real

landscape, Gainsborough's use of small models as compositional aids is not nearly as intrusive here as it would occasionally be later, largely because of the extraordinary unification of the composition. Oddly, it is when Gainsborough is attempting to invent simpler, more naturalistic scenery that the weaknesses of his table-top construction are most apparent; for example, in *A Mountain Valley with Rustic Figures, a Shepherd and Sheep and a Distant Village and Mountains* (page 103). The technique was better suited to more decorative arrangements.

Although Gainsborough's landscapes may have been avidly collected by friends such as Thicknesse and Wollaston, the genre had as yet no place in the popular conception of what constituted 'great art'. Most landscapes were straightforwardly topographical or charmingly decorative, and a landscapist's skill was considered important chiefly for providing convincing or impressive settings for paintings of Biblical or historical subjects and, of course, for the backgrounds of the more expensive portraits. Even in Gainsborough's portraits we can detect an overriding interest in landscape; look, for example, at the care he

Peasants with Cattle by a Stream in a Woody Landscape
('The Watering Place') *by Rubens, c.1615–22.*
Black chalk and oil on wood, approx 98.7 × 135 cm
National Gallery, London

has lavished on the background of *General Johnston*. In his mature portraits he comes to use landscape, often in a highly generalized manner, to suggest rather than signify directly the status of his sitter. Thus, while it was usual to portray an admiral by the sea or a soldier on the battlefield, Gainsborough often used subtle variations on a basic rural or Arcadian setting to suggest a mood rather than to spell out the precise social circumstances of his client. The finest example of this is to be found in his portrait of *Mrs Richard Brinsley Sheridan* (page 121), where he has used the same palette for the subject's dress and surroundings, and a uniform system of brushwork to unify subject and setting; in this way he has created not so much a scene as an atmosphere.

Gainsborough's development of the landscape genre coincided with, and was undoubtedly encouraged by the sea change in public attitudes to art in Britain; a change that witnessed the setting-up and development of institutions devoted to the study and promotion of art which survive largely unchanged to this day. Until the 1760s, paintings of any size or contemporary significance were only produced on commission, whether private or, like Captain Coram's Foundling Hospital, more or less public. Artists might produce small works, particularly engravings and drawings, and sell them to dealers, but there was almost no public exhibition of paintings, as there was on the Continent. The exhibition which Hogarth organized of the works produced for the Foundling Hospital proved so popular, however, that various exhibiting societies and professional clubs were founded in response, and out of these grew the Society of Artists, which held its first exhibition in 1760. Gainsborough submitted a picture the following year, a portrait of Lord Nugent, and in 1763 he sent a landscape – possibly the *Grand Landscape* mentioned earlier. Thereafter he sent two or three pictures a year, almost all of them portraits.

One of the main benefits of the Society of Artists' annual exhibitions was the rapid rise of a British school of art criticism, at first centred on newspapers and magazines and later – as the discipline matured – in published collections of essays and theoretical theses. Art, and *new* art in particular, was suddenly fashionable, an appropriate subject for discussion among the intelligentsia and the 'chattering classes'. The relative merits of Reynolds and Ramsay and later of Reynolds and Gainsborough, and which painters were being patronized by the arbiters of fashion (and by the Royal Family) became subjects of intense debate and gossip. Journalists, critics and intellectuals chose and fought for their favourites, often vitriolically; William Blake went so far as to remark that Reynolds had been 'Hired to Depress Art' and spoke of Reynolds's 'gang of . . . Knaves'.

Much attention focused on the relationship between the leading figures of the theatrical world – who occupied much the same kind of social position as movie stars do today – and the new 'stars' of portraiture. The London stage was enjoying one of its most glorious periods, with David Garrick and Sarah Siddons its two leading lights. Garrick and Gainsborough became close friends (though Gainsborough was disappointed with the portrait – since destroyed – he painted of the actor for Mrs Garrick). Of Gainsborough, Garrick remarked that, 'His cranium is so crammed with genius of every kind that it is in danger of bursting upon you, like a steam engine overcharged.' The phrase 'genius of every kind' is a telling one. Gainsborough thrust himself into this glittering world of actors, intellectuals and aristocrats. Contemporary accounts stress his talents not just as an artist but as a musician, conversationalist and wit. His writing, limited though it was to long, meandering and often confessional letters to his friends (and sometimes terse ones to his patrons), was considered by one acquaintance to be on a par with that of Laurence Sterne, whose huge rambling comic novel *Tristram Shandy* was one of the great contemporary successes. Gainsborough found himself at dinner tables with the likes not only of Garrick but also Dr Johnson, Richard Brinsley Sheridan, Beau Nash, the astronomer Herschel and similar luminaries. The concept of genius, of the fully-rounded man, is one of the key ideas which arose in the arts at this time. It was not limited, as in the more modern sense, to a particular skill, but had a much broader connotation, and was as much a condition of the mind as a whole as it was a specific talent. Gainsborough, who on occasion displayed a distinct nervousness at being fêted in company, and at finding himself out of his depth, would often turn the conversation away at a tangent by a witty disparaging remark, particularly if literature or the classics were being discussed. Far from it being held against him, however, this apparent ignorance was regarded as evidence of an unusually lively intellect coupled with a becoming modesty. In fact, he had a happy knack of grasping subjects intuitively rather than intellectually and was rarely, if ever, wrong-footed by his comparative lack of formal education. His friend William Jackson of Exeter recalled that:

His conversation was sprightly, but licentious – his favourite subjects were music and painting; which he treated in a manner peculiarly his own. The common topics, or any of a superior cast, he thoroughly hated, and always interrupted by some stroke of wit or humour . . . so far from writing, [he] scarcely ever read a book – but for a letter . . . he had few equals and no superior. It was like his conversation; gay, lively – fluttering round subjects which he just touched, and away to another.

Another acquaintance speaks of Gainsborough's almost manic conversation as they were out walking, continually pointing things out, making jokes or sarcastic quips about passers-by, touching on apparently unconnected subjects brought to mind by chance sights and sounds; an experience at once exhilarating and exhausting. Gainsborough hated cant and what he regarded as the unnecessarily exaggerated displays of courtesy displayed when gentlemen called upon him at his studio. He left firm instructions that unless they seemed very keen to buy they should be turned away – although to turn away

Johann Christian Bach, 1776.
Oil on canvas, 75 × 62 cm
Bologna, Civico Museo Bibliografico Musicale

women was 'more than my life is worth'. This straightforwardness may be one reason why he scrupulously avoided history painting and the kind of classical allusions favoured by portraitists such as Reynolds. At the height of his success he became a great favourite of the Royal Family and produced many portraits of them. He clearly felt at ease with royalty and they with him, once jokingly telling a friend that he 'talked bawdy to the King and morality to the Prince of Wales'.

As at Ipswich, he quickly became an indispensable guest at any fashionable gathering, from the formal concerts and musical soirées at the spa, to private balls and concert parties. As his financial situation improved, he was able to indulge his passion for music and for musical instruments, buying a great many or exchanging paintings for them. His range of contacts and acquaintances grew apace, and the social standing of his customers rose dramatically. There is little doubt that Gainsborough's success at Bath had more than a little to do with his personal charm and affability and the vagaries of fashion, and many writers have seen the influence of Philip Thicknesse behind this rapid transformation into the most modish artist of the day. Thicknesse worked tirelessly on his behalf in the first few years of the Bath period, but the two men became estranged before Gainsborough left for London, for reasons which neither Gainsborough's correspondence nor Thicknesse's memoirs make clear. The most likely explanation is that Thicknesse found himself in financial difficulties and became a burden, and there are hints that Margaret, Gainsborough's wife, disliked him intensely. Certainly, Thicknesse, who had a very short fuse and was decidedly eccentric, if not actually deranged, was not above petty blackmail; and Gainsborough, who by his own admission led a fairly debauched existence (by no means uncommon at the time), was undoubtedly tormented by his own weaknesses and keen to keep them hidden from his wife. In 1763 he was so ill, probably with syphilis, that the *Bath Journal* actually announced his death. His wife nursed him devotedly throughout five weeks in bed, and afterwards he wrote in a letter to Jackson, 'O, my dear Friend, nobody can think what I have suffer'd for a Moments Gratification . . . my dear good wife has sat up every night . . . I will never be a quarter good enough for her if I mend a hundred degrees.'

Margaret remains a shadowy personality. It is evident that their relationship was often severely strained, and not only by her husband's sexual adventures. She seems to have been obsessively thrifty, and even when Gainsborough was earning a considerable sum (as he did from the early 1760s), she retained a firm grip on the purse strings. We find him apologizing to a customer for charging a few shillings for the packing case on top of the fee for the painting itself because, as he explains, his wife would not forgive him if he forgot. If he took a cab rather than walking home, he would pay the driver off around the corner from the house so that Margaret did not see. And he was not above arranging sales of his paintings without her knowledge, and putting the money straight into his own pocket. Another bone of contention was Gainsborough's remarkably – even ridiculously – generous nature. He frequently gave away paintings to friends. On one occasion he was going to the opera with a friend who, on the way there, told him a hard-luck story about a woman acquaintance. Although he seems not to have known the woman in question, Gainsborough went straight home and sent her a bank note, explaining that he could not have enjoyed the opera otherwise. On another occasion he borrowed twenty pounds – then a considerable sum – from his sister Mary to give to 'a poor wench', as he did not dare ask his wife. Of course, this is open to an interpretation other than sheer generosity: when Margaret and the children were packed off to stay with the Kilderbees in Suffolk one summer, Gainsborough records that they returned unexpectedly early, as 'Madam is afraid to trust me alone at home in this great Town.' Not without reason, it would seem. He resorted eventually to storing his landscapes out of sight, away from the studio, and keeping their prices secret; however, Margaret was well aware of the going rate for portraits. Commenting on their relationship, Thicknesse once remarked bitterly that 'those who best loved Mr Gainsborough, and whom he most loved, were unfortunately least welcome in his house.'

Apart from the stresses on his marriage, and his own debauches – his younger daughter Margaret said that he 'often exceeded the bounds of temperance and his Health suffered from it, being occasionally unable to work for a week afterwards' – Gainsborough soon found that he had an additional worry. When his younger daughter was nineteen she fell seriously ill with a mental condition which was a consequence of her inherited syphilis. Gainsborough was extremely fond of his daughters, nicknamed Molly and The Captain, and it is evident that he suffered great private anguish over this sad episode. Although Margaret recovered, she continued to show signs of instability throughout her life. Mary, the older sister, seems to have been relatively untroubled as a young woman, but towards the end of her life became completely mad, believing amongst other things that the Prince of Wales was in love with her.

In their twenties both daughters became besotted with the eminent musician Johann Christian Fischer, a frequent guest at Gainsborough's musical evenings. Fischer was invited by virtue of his musicianship only and Gainsborough, thinking him vain and stupid, was worried lest Fischer propose to Margaret. It came as a shock, therefore, when 'the other slyboots' became engaged to him; but he put a brave face on it and was doubtless relieved to see his daughter married. Later in the year he painted a fine portrait of Fischer, so they were presumably on speaking terms (page 115). The marriage lasted only a few months: 'Fischer has deceived me in his Circumstances and [Mary] has been playing the Devil to raise Money', he wrote. Mary returned home, and Margaret never married. After their parents' deaths, both daughters lapsed into an increasingly eccentric and lonely, though financially secure existence, with Margaret doing her level best to keep her deranged sister out of harm's way. Gainsborough's own marriage survived intact, as testified by his tender portrait of his wife, painted around 1779 when she was about fifty (page 111).

The Gainsboroughs' closest friends in Bath were the Linley family, who were near neighbours famed for their musical talents. Thomas Linley was an impresario as well as an instrumentalist; his son Tom was a prodigy for whom Mozart had predicted a glittering career, and Elizabeth and Mary, the two daughters, were talented singers (page 99). Elizabeth, who caused an enormous scandal by eloping with Richard Sheridan, was the subject of perhaps the finest of all Gainsborough's portraits (page 121).

Apart from the social whirl (which he professed to dislike) Gainsborough's chief amusements at Bath were riding, which weather permitting he did every day, and, as usual, sketching in the countryside. He was a frequent guest at Foxley, the home of Uvedale Tomkins Price (page 79), his son Robert and his grandson, also called Uvedale, who later wrote an influential treatise on the Picturesque. Several drawings and sketches of trees, fences and other details at Foxley survive. He also copied Old Masters when he could, sometimes attempting a straight copy and then a freer version in his own style. As he grew richer, Gainsborough was able to move into an even more fashionable address in The Circus, the great circular 'square' which is the chief architectural glory of the city and was then the hub of Bath society. By the late 1760s he had become, due to this ideally visible position and to the exhibitions of the Society of Artists, a figure of national fame, and able to attract sitters such as Mary, Duchess of Montagu from the highest echelons of society. Indeed the list of his portraits of the period bristles with Admirals, Generals, Dukes, Earls, Marquises and Viscountesses, as well as business people like John Wilkinson and James Christie. As the Montagu portrait testifies, Gainsborough was never one to flatter his sitters. He painted exactly what he saw. There is always a suspicion that other portraitists of the time did their best to conceal the physical shortcomings of their clients, particularly young women – Reynolds shows a distinct tendency to classicize their facial characteristics as well as dress and setting. Gainsborough must be credited for resisting this, and in Mary Montagu's portrait (page 93) we can glimpse what his admirers meant when they praised his ability to catch a likeness – he painted character as much as appearance.

The picture which perhaps exemplifies the confidence which Gainsborough had gained by this time is the so-called 'Blue Boy', a portrait of Jonathan Buttall (page 97). He is dressed in a studio-prop Van Dyck costume which Gainsborough used more than once. The picture is an homage to the heroic portraiture of

Anne, Countess of Clanbrassil
by Sir Anthony Van Dyck, 1636.
Oil on canvas, 212.1 × 127.6 cm
Copyright The Frick Collection, New York

the great Dutch artist, but is by no means a straight pastiche. Whereas Van Dyck's full-lengths are sedate, often aloof and superior, the Blue Boy is an image of great romanticism, engaging and direct. Just as Hogarth broke with convention in *Captain Coram* (see page 12), Gainsborough has taken the language of the heroic military portrait (the costume is reminis-

cent of the Civil War) and applied it to an unknown, if very good-looking, middle-class boy – Jonathan Buttall was the son of an ironmonger in Soho. As Waterhouse remarked, Gainsborough had grafted 'all the elegance [of] Van Dyck onto his own native style'. The picture caused a sensation when it was shown in London. Mary Moser, one of the two women founder-members of the Royal Academy, wrote to Fuseli that 'Gainsborough is beyond himself', and his old teacher Hayman thought it as good as Van Dyck himself. Perhaps the greatest lesson Gainsborough learned from Van Dyck was how to construct a full-length so that the image would best impress the viewer – using a low perspective so that the figure seems to tower over us. There is nothing threatening or bombastic here, but this technique adds immeasurably to the immediacy and power of the image.

Oddly enough, Gainsborough professed a dislike of the fashion for using antique costume in portraiture. Indeed, he wrote to one client:

Nothing can be more absurd than the foolish custom of Painters dressing people like scaramouches and expecting a likeness to appear; had a picture Voice, action, &c, to make itself known as Actors have upon the Stage, no disguise would be sufficient to conceal a person, but only a face confined to one View and not a muscle to move to say here I am falls very hard upon the poor Painter . . . I defy any but a Painter of some sagacity (and such you see I am my Lord) to be well aware of the different Effects which one part of the picture has upon the other, and how the Eye may be cheated as to the appearance of Size etc., by the artful management of the accompanyments . . . a hansom Face [shall] be overset by a ficticious bundle of trumpery of the foolish painter's own inventing.

This is a most curious tirade, given Gainsborough's predeliction for enormously showy and complicated swathes of silks and satins. Though he never resorted to the kind of Graeco-Roman robes that Reynolds and later Lawrence draped over their aristocratic sitters, he clearly did not attempt to play down in the

Mrs Henry Baring and her Children
by Sir Thomas Lawrence, begun 1817.
Oil on canvas, 194.3 × 195.6 cm
Courtesy of the Directors of Barings

slightest the tremendously showy dresses of his richest clients, though he could be direct in his criticism, telling Sarah Siddons to go out and buy a new hat. And despite the fact that these particular bundles of trumpery were not ficticious it would be an exaggeration to say that they do not, on occasion, deflect our attention away from the visage of the sitter.

What might best be described as Gainsborough's new-found ability to manipulate the 'atmosphere' of his portraits, as in *The Blue Boy*, is demonstrated once again in his picture of the Linley sisters, where modesty and cool refinement in keeping with their age and 'public image' as performers is suggested (page 99). This preoccupation with the total effect of the portrait was to result later in a famous argument with the Hanging Committee of the Academy. He had come a long way from the simple portrayal of figures like the Andrews and Plampin, where a likeness is the

overriding preoccupation. Though he often uses the simplest sort of setting for his sitters in Bath and London – John Wilkinson's is typical – and though in portraits such as that of *The Hon. Mrs Graham* (page 107) he uses a completely conventional scenery no more believable than a nineteenth-century photographer's backdrop, from the mid-1760s he never produces a portrait which does not work as a complete picture. In particular he uses colours in his scenery and skies which echo those in the sitter's costume, or to compliment them, and he was adept at constructing a picture geometrically so as to lead the eye, often via a series of curves, away from and back to the figure so that it is impossible not to appreciate the canvas as a whole. His sometimes almost violent brushwork amplifies this, 'binding' the figure to the rest of the work.

Not all his best work was so formal, however, as the 'snapshot' effect of the *Pitminster Boy* – an unknown sitter – shows. This kind of highly informal work had been popularized by Hogarth; his *Shrimp Girl* being a well-known example.

From the new sophistication of the Worcester *Grand Landscape* (page 81) Gainsborough's landscape work takes off in a series of ambitious and varied experiments. One of the most obvious innovations is a willingness to bring figures from an incidental to a central position within these works. Whereas in such works as the *Extensive River Landscape* of 1753 or 1754 in Edinburgh (page 119) the figures are designed to punctuate and humanize what is essentially a picture of scenery, many later works can really be described as pictures in which the human dramatic subject comes first, with the scenery, much as in the portraits, playing an amplificatory role. Once again, Gainsborough attacks this new concern with bravado; the wonderfully fluid articulation of limbs as the woman is helped into *The Harvest Waggon* (page 89) is in fact borrowed from Rubens's *Deposition* at Wilton House, though not very directly. *The Woodcutter's Return* (page 101) is another example, though it marks something of a return to the Dutch tradition. Somewhere between the two, the *Wooded Landscape with Country Waggon, Milkmaid and Drover* (page 87) of 1766 represents an attempt to balance the kind of 'human interest' seen earlier in the Ruisdael-influenced Woburn landscape (page 65) with the kind of highly romantic scenery first seen in the Worcester picture of 1763. And there is a fine rare topographical scene, the *View near King's Bromley* (page 95), which is an extraordinary composition and closer to the approach of John Constable in his paintings of the Stour than it is to the Dutch tradition.

In 1768 his old friend Joshua Kirby wrote to him asking his support for, and offering him a Directorship of the Society of Artists, of which Kirby (a mediocre painter) was President. But Gainsborough

Portrait of an Unknown Youth,
('The Pitminster Boy'),
later 1760s.
Oil on canvas, 58.4 × 50.8 cm
Private Collection

had already been asked to become a founder-member of the Royal Academy of Arts, which had been set up to provide the first-rate School of Art Britain so sorely lacked. The Society of Artists had been an exhibiting society primarily; now the R.A. was to take away that function also, and Gainsborough had to refuse Kirby's request. Joshua Reynolds was the first President of the Academy, and the personal antipathy between Gainsborough and Reynolds had its roots in this time, although it was by Reynolds's invitation that Gainsborough joined. There was no longer any doubt that these were the two leading portraitists of the day; Ramsay's work had declined, becoming repetitious and dated. When Gainsborough moved from Bath to London in 1774 the rivalry intensified dramatically.

The immediate reasons for Gainsborough's departure from Bath are not known, though Thicknesse claims it was due to a row with his wife Ann over an unfinished portrait of himself. Only a complete egomaniac could imagine that a painter of Gainsborough's stature would move house over such a matter, and the explanation seems to be that Gainsborough's business in Bath was in decline. It may be that he had priced himself out of the market – he was charging a hundred guineas for a full-length by the early 1770s, and received three times as much on occasion. (Reynolds, ever conscious of his reputation, was charging a hundred and fifty.) Or perhaps Bath was not quite the epicentre it once had been. When Joseph Wright of Derby arrived there shortly afterwards he found he could attract only one significant customer in his first two seasons, though it must be said that Wright was never in the same league as Gainsborough in the eyes of the public or of his fellow-artists; charming though some of his portraits are, they exhibit an unusual individualism (*Brooke Boothby*, for instance). There is also some reason to suppose that Gainsborough was no longer quite the dashingly fashionable figure he once was – he had after all been a professional for almost three decades and had been in the spotlight for almost twenty years. But apart from these reasons it may be that to some

Sir Brooke Boothby,
by Joseph Wright of Derby, 1781.
Oil on canvas, 148.6 × 207.6 cm
Courtesy of the Tate Gallery, London

extent Gainsborough, whose landscapes had rapidly come to popularity and who was shortly to score another great success with his 'Fancy pictures', deliberately moved himself out of a position in which he was under pressure to produce a large number of portraits, which he found increasingly tedious.

Gainsborough's London home, Schomberg House, Pall Mall, was just as fashionable as his Bath address had been. He was by now earning a considerable sum annually – probably over 20,000 guineas – but records that his expenses were high. Not only did he have two grown daughters still at home but, at least for a while, a footman and a coachman, as well as stables and a carriage to maintain. These were soon shed, however, and he even managed to put aside a tidy little sum in government bonds, probably at Margaret's insistence. He also had a cottage at fashionable Richmond, where he would go to rest and enjoy the river and its surrounding countryside.

Gainsborough's old friend Sir Joshua Kirby died shortly after the artist's arrival in London. They had

been on very good terms, despite Gainsborough's electing to join the Royal Academy rather than the Society of Artists, and Gainsborough told his wife that on his death he wished to be buried at Kew alongside Kirby. Thereafter the most important figure of influence was another man of the cloth, the Reverend (later Sir) Henry Bate-Dudley, who wrote many supportive articles on Gainsborough's work for the *Morning Post*. The two probably met through the actor David Garrick: it was Bate-Dudley who had encouraged Garrick to go and see an unknown actress by the name of Sarah Siddons.

If one of the possible reasons for Gainsborough's departure from Bath was the decline in demand for his work, a certain credibility is given to this by the fact that in London he seems initially to have been under-employed (since he was now charging several hundred guineas for his largest works, the number of potential clients was greatly reduced). Anxious for work, he accepted the offer of his two friends, Karl Abel and Johann Christian Bach (see pages 36 and 30), to decorate their new music rooms in Hanover Square. This led to another important meeting, with Philip de Loutherbourg.

De Loutherbourg became Gainsborough's closest friend, and the two seem to have had much in common. Indeed, de Loutherbourg seems to have been in many ways a kindred spirit. He was a talented musician, a painter of some skill if not originality, and an inventor. He had designed an early magic lantern, the Eidophusikon, which was one of the great popular successes of London society. It was in effect a miniature theatre, lit by candles and using glass slides painted with figures and scenery. Gainsborough, perhaps because of his brother 'Scheming Jack', was fascinated by all things mechanical, and the two men put on shows with it, complete with sound effects. (He is said to have cried 'Our thunder is the best!' after one show.) Gainsborough later built his own 'magic box' on much the same basis, now in the Victoria & Albert Museum, London.

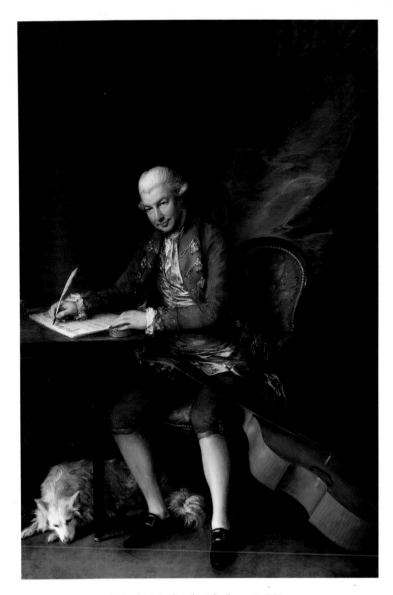

Karl Friedrich Abel, c.1777.
Oil on canvas, 223.5 × 147.3 cm
The Huntington Art Collections, San Marino

If Gainsborough did have time on his hands after 1774, it had no detrimental effects on his work, for from this time onwards he produced not only his finest landscape paintings and arguably the greatest series of portraits of that century, but also a type of picture new to him, his so-called 'Fancy pictures'. In works such as *The Cottage Door* and *The Market Cart* (pages 113 and 133) we see the culmination of Gainsborough's attempts to create a landscape genre in which the kind of rural idyll expressed in contemporary poetry and literature is displayed in works

which do not merely set out anecdotal scenes of Arcadian country life, but do so in a way that demands as much attention to the construction of the picture as to the scenery and incidents portrayed. This was a completely new phenomenon in British art, and one which had arguably the most lasting influence on painting thereafter. Although the relationship is not a direct one, the similarity of intention between a picture such as *The Market Cart* and Constable's *The Haywain*, for example, is obvious. Constable was always much more directly concerned with naturalism, and although his landscapes often contain an element of human interest, his characters are always more directly linked to reality than Gainsborough's forest dwellers, milkmaids and swains. Constable's country folk do real work – they pull barges and harvest crops – and they derive more directly from the work of George Stubbs than from Gainsborough. Gainsborough painted essentially imaginary scenes, but this makes him only different to, not less honest than Constable. He was concerned not with naturalistic, but with poetic representation. Gainsborough's landscape art did, however, have a powerful influence on later painting, particularly during the Victorian era, when scenes of idealized country life became, in the hands of painters such as Landseer and Millais, the staple fare of the Royal Academy Summer Exhibitions, though with a considerably stronger anecdotal and sentimental emphasis than Gainsborough's work.

Ironically it was the 'Fancy pictures' – which now seem to us amongst Gainsborough's weakest productions – that generated most critical acclaim. Again, the overwhelming popularity of this type of picture during the nineteenth century to some extent blinds us to the effect they must have had on Gainsborough's public, who it appears were astonished by them. Joshua Reynolds said that *The Girl with Pigs* was the finest work this artist had ever done – and paid 100 guineas for it. Gainsborough wrote to say that he was glad his pigs had come to 'so fair a market'. Despite their disagreements, the two men had a healthy respect for each other's talents; Gainsborough once

The Girl with Pigs, *c.1782*.
Oil on canvas, 152.4 × 129.4 cm
From the Castle Howard Collection

wrote, clearly envious, upon seeing a brilliant new picture by Reynolds, 'Damn him, how various he is!'

For his fancy pictures, such as *The Cottage Girl* (page 127), Gainsborough often employed as models chil-

dren he met while out walking. He also brought into his studio any items he felt might contribute to the success of the picture – large branches, donkeys, dogs, and, in the case of *The Girl with Pigs*, a number of pigs, which roamed Schomberg House for several days. Gainsborough would have known works like Greuze's *The Broken Pitcher*, with its mawkish sexual symbolism, from engravings. *The Cottage Girl*, though considerably less cloying, would appear closely indebted to Greuze's work.

There is no doubt, however, that for all his moaning – 'If the People with their damn'd faces would but let me alone' – Gainsborough's greatest work was the series of portraits made between 1774 and 1788. Perhaps because he could by now afford to be fussy, and had more time to spend on each, they are superior even to the best of his Bath pictures. Even those which are strictly conventional in their setting, such as *The Hon. Mrs Graham* and *The Hon. Frances Duncombe* (pages 107 and 109), are extraordinarily sumptuous. Reynolds at his finest never approaches this sheer density and complexity of work. Gainsborough used paint so thin that it dripped off his palette if he did not hold it straight, adding layer upon layer of translucent strokes to build up not only the exquisite texture of his sitters' dresses but their rich, vibrant colouring. As a result of this technique they are today in marvellous condition, far fresher than Reynolds's portraits, which have faded and discoloured badly.

To his credit – given his profound boredom with society portraiture – Gainsborough was at this time still experimenting. Perhaps the most striking of all these London pictures, *Mr and Mrs William Hallett*, known popularly as *The Morning Walk* (page 131), combines the tradition of the marriage portrait with the poise and glamour characteristic of his depictions of fashionable lady sitters. One has only to compare it with *Mrs and Mrs Andrews* or *The Byam Family* (pages 55 and 85) to realize the astonishing growth in Gainsborough's ambition and technical ability over the years. Nothing is fudged or glossed over in this picture; every tiny detail, from the cloudscape to the highlights on the buttons, from the slight wrinkle on the knee of Mr Hallett's stocking to the buckle on his wife's shoe, testifies not only to a prodigious feat of concentration but, despite Gainsborough's complaints, to a sheer enjoyment in the painting process itself. This type of close, minute work might in the hands of a less skilled painter have resulted in an almost hallucinatory, hyper-real effect, and his greatest achievement in this sizeable painting is the completely unified texture, the unvarying softness of

The Broken Pitcher
by Jean-Baptiste Greuze, 1773.
Oil on canvas
Musée du Louvre, Paris

the image. Despite its extravagant complexity, the effect is one of calmness and urbanity.

In 1772, whilst still living in Bath, Gainsborough had quarrelled with the Royal Academy over a picture he had sent up to the annual Summer Exhibition, a portrait of the Countess of Waldegrave. The Countess, rather indiscreetly, had been conducting an affair with the Duke of Gloucester, the brother of King George III, and Reynolds, as President of the Academy, forbad the picture to be hung for fear of offending the King. Gainsborough was incensed by the decision, which he no doubt attributed to professional jealousy, and sent no pictures for five years (although he was elected to the Council of the Academy in 1774). Gainsborough seems often to have been insensitive to the finer feelings of his clients and his public – or perhaps he regarded such matters as mere hypocrisy. In 1778 he sent up several portraits to the Academy, causing a great palaver because two were of well-known courtesans, Clara Haywood and Grace Dalrymple, who were hung shoulder to shoulder, as it were, with the likes of the Duchess of Devonshire. In 1782 he caused a similar scandal by sending a portrait of Mrs Perdita Robinson, the mistress of the Prince of Wales, which he withdrew after a strongly critical article in a newspaper, (Reynolds, ironically, allowed his own portrait of her to be shown).

Despite these interruptions, Gainsborough's work continued to find great critical favour: 'one steps back for fear of being splashed', wrote Horace Walpole of his coastal scenes, and described another painting as 'the most beautiful [landscape] which has ever been painted in England and equal to the great masters.' He continued to avoid History painting completely and, on reading Reynolds's fourth *Discourse to the Academy*, complained that 'Sir Joshua either forgets, or does not chuse [sic] to see that his Instruction is all adapted to form the History Painter, which he must know there is no call for in this country.' Reynolds remarked in his turn that Gainsborough had 'a painter's eye but not a painter's mind'. In actual fact Reynolds probably underestimated Gainsborough's intellectual capacity, as at the end of his life he had finally plucked up courage to embark on a large painting of a mythological subject, *Diana and Actaeon* (page 139), which was left incomplete, but which promised a great deal. Gainsborough was also fond, as John Hayes points out, of adapting 'high' subjects to his own ends; several of his landscapes are 'rusticated' versions of Claudian or Poussinesque themes. But above all Gainsborough was wise enough not to try and compete with Reynolds on his own territory: 'you know my cunning way of avoiding great subjects in Painting and of concealing my

ignorance with a Flash in the Pan', he wrote to his friend Sir William Chambers.

The quarrels with the Royal Academy Hanging Committee rumbled on; in 1783 he sent up a number of portraits of the Royal Family that he had been invited to paint at Windsor the previous year. As usual the Academy ignored his express wishes as to how they were to be displayed – instructions which, as a member of the Council and currently one of the two finest painters in Britain, he was surely entitled to expect would be heeded. He submitted the works accompanied by a note saying,

Mr Gainsborough presents his Compliments to the Gentlemen appointed to hang the Pictures at the Royal Academy; and begs leave to hint to Them, that if the Royal Family . . . are hung above the line along with full lengths he never more, whilst he breaths, will send another Picture to the Exhibition – this he swears by God.

He got his way, but the following year fell out completely over the hanging of a picture of the three eldest princesses:

Mr Gainsborough's Compts to the Gentn of the Committee and begs pardon for giving them so much trouble; but he has painted this Picture of the Princesses in so tender a light, that notwithstanding he approves very much of the established line for Strong Effects [i.e. the line above which full-lengths were usually hung, above door level] he cannot possibly consent to have it placed higher than five feet and a half, because the likenesses and work of the picture will not be seen any higher; therefore at a word, he will not trouble the Gentlemen against their Inclination, but will beg the rest of his pictures back again.

The urbane language barely conceals his fury – the 'rest of his pictures' included *The Mall* (page 123), commissioned by the king, and sixteen others. He exhibited them all at Schomberg House instead, and never showed at the Academy thereafter, preferring annually to hang his own shows. Note Gainsborough's emphasis on 'likeness' and the 'Work'; 'effect' is all very well, he implies, but he wanted his picture to be properly examined at close range to display his technical facility.

Gainsborough evidently enjoyed a close relationship with George III, Queen Charlotte, and their thirteen children. Apart from the portraits he received several other commissions, and it is thought that surviving sketches of two fashionable women were preliminary studies for a large painting commissioned by the king in the style of *The Mall*, to be entitled *The Richmond Water Walk*. He did not, however, do them any financial favours, charging them the going rate and more for his time. Understandably, he entertained some hope of being appointed Principal Painter to the King on the death of Ramsay in 1784, but Reynolds was given the position. Although it was largely a symbolic, prestige post rather than a lucrative one, Gainsborough was evidently disappointed, having perhaps thought that his close acquaintance with the Royal Family – in contrast with Reynolds's unpopularity with them – would have secured him the job. He refers rather darkly to internal politicking at the Academy, but as Reynolds was the first President of an academy founded by the king, the position could hardly have been given to anyone else.

As Gainsborough approached his sixtieth year, his work continued undiminished in either quality or quantity – indeed, still gaining in the former at least. He made a sketching tour of the Lake District in 1783, but did not produce any topographical oil paintings as a result (though a surviving letter suggests that he intended to). His life of bursts of hard work interrupted by periods of carousing, music-making and country retreats continued unchanged.

In the *Self-portrait* of 1787 (page 135), produced during his sixtieth year, we see, apparently, a confident, secure man with a level gaze and a slightly wry expression. He seems to have worn well. But in March 1788 he complained of a lump in his neck

Studies of a Cat, *c.1765–69.*
Black chalk, stump and white chalk on buff paper,
31 × 44.7 cm
Rijksmuseum, Amsterdam

which grew more painful by the day. He was fairly sure that it was a cancerous tumour, and this proved to be the case. It was, of course, inoperable; cancer in those days was a death sentence. He made a will during the summer.

He seems to have borne the disease lightly despite the severe pain: 'Hope is the pallat colours we all paint with in sickness', he wrote, 'I feel such a fondness for my first imitations of little Dutch landskips . . . I am so childish I could make a kite, catch gold finches or build little ships.' He still managed to paint for a couple of hours daily, until he was exhausted by the pain. A few weeks before his death, he wrote to Sir Joshua Reynolds one of his most moving letters:

Dear Sir Joshua, I am just to write what I fear you will not read after lying in a dying state for 6 months. The extreme affection which I am informed of by a Friend which Sir Joshua has expresd induces me to beg one last Favour, which is to come once under my Roof and look at my things; my Woodman you never saw, if what I ask is not disagreeable to you feeling that I may have the honour to speak to you. I can from a sincere Heart say that I always admired and sincerely loved Sir Joshua Reynolds.

Reynolds came and, as he related in his next *Discourse*, devoted entirely to Gainsborough's work, the two men forgot their 'little jealousies': 'he [Gainsborough] turned towards me as one who was engrossed by the same pursuits and who deserved his good opinion by being sensible of his excellencies.' Samuel Kilderbee also came to see him, and was told by the dying man, 'They must take me altogether – liberal, thoughtless and dissipated.' According to his daughter Margaret, however, his last words were 'We are all going to Heaven and Van Dyck is of the company.' He died on 2 August 1788, and was, as requested, buried next to Joshua Kirby in Kew churchyard.

Gainsborough's portraits, being of fashionable people, went out of fashion quickly after his death. His widow held a number of sales of his remaining works, but many pictures failed to find buyers or went for far less than she had hoped. Still, she lived comfortably enough, as did her daughters, until she died in 1798. Gainsborough's landscape work remained popular, but his portraits did not come back into critical favour until the beginning of the twentieth century, when the great Edwardian portraitists such as John Singer Sargent were producing their own opulent pictures of fashionable society men and women. His fancy pictures found favour in Victorian times but have probably lost their original potency forever, as we are no longer able to appreciate them as Gainsborough intended, bombarded as we are by images too similar and too calculatedly sentimental.

Gainsborough is not an artist who can be pigeonholed into a convenient art-historical niche. His talents were too various and his work too personal for that.

Nevertheless, he was by no means an outsider and to understand him fully one needs a far more intimate knowledge of eighteenth-century society than can be provided here. There seems little doubt that parts of the key to his enigma are his sociability and his social mobility – one has a strong feeling that the late eighteenth century's liberalism, its radical realignment of attitudes to social class, allowed his career to flourish in a way that could not have happened either fifty years earlier or fifty years later. Earlier, and he would not have been able to escape his rural roots; later, and Reynolds's academic legacy would have completely reshaped his art. As it was, he was allowed to be himself, to make his own rules.

Art history has always had to balance nature and culture, individual and society, in its account of artists' work. Gainsborough's art typifies this dilemma, for while his social background and apparently direct portrayal of society provide tempting material for an account of his career based on a materialist analysis, the biographical information which survives, scanty though it is, makes an unusually powerful case for the individualist cause. He was a magnetic and charismatic man, a charmer and a humourist. Most appealing of all, he had a sound sense of his own limitations and a distrust of the tendency of artists and critics to mystify their trade. One of the most frequently quoted appraisals of his works is by Constable: 'The landscape of Gainsborough is soothing, tender and affecting . . . [on looking at] the canvases of this most benevolent and kind-hearted man . . . we find tears in our eyes, and know not what brings them.' Gainsborough, however, might have appreciated a less lachrymose epitaph, such as this remark by Dunning: 'He puts no more motion than what goes into the real performance, which constitute that ease and gentility peculiar to damn'd clever Fellows.'

Gainsborough.

THE PLATES

This, one of Gainsborough's earliest surviving works, raises a number of tantalizing questions. Although in the Dutch landscape style and particularly close to the work of Johannes Wijnants, it is rather freer in handling. Does this indicate that at this time Gainsborough was consciously attempting to assert his own style, or simply that the picture was done quickly? It is in fact finished? If the painting was intended to be 'after Wijnants' then we would expect the foreground to be more crisply painted, with something of the solidity of the trees behind the cottage. Much of the surface is only very thinly coated, with the canvas almost showing through in places, and the green sward in the middle distance consists of a single thin coat of translucent paint. Details such as the ladder leaning against the thatch of the cottage seem also to have been left merely sketched in, in contrast to the thick white impasto of the chalk bank and the sheep's wool.

Gainsborough was perhaps only seventeen years old and still studying in London when he painted this landscape, which accounts for its strongly derivative nature. There are, however, signs of his potential. Although the overall design is rather weak and the perspective not wholly satisfactory, the handling of the play of light on the left-hand foreground of the picture is confident, and the white wall of the cottage against the dark trees prefigures some similarly eye-catching passages in the landscapes of the next few years; for example, in *A View in Suffolk* (page 49).

This type of picture would have found a ready market, particularly in East Anglia, where Dutch landscape work was then still very popular.

Crossing the Ford

Painted c.1744–5
32.4 × 35.9 cm
The National Trust, Upton House

We do not know the circumstances under which this charming little picture was commissioned, but it was almost certainly painted at Sudbury during one of Gainsborough's frequent visits home from his studies in London, and it is likely that the Hills – who owned Bumper – were friends of the Gainsborough family.

It was common for the landed gentry and aristocracy to commission portraits of their favourite animals – particularly their horses and dogs – and several eighteenth-century painters, most notably George Stubbs, supported themselves largely through such work. Gainsborough's inexperience in the genre is clear, and the overall impression is one of naïvety, particularly in the awkwardness of scale caused by an insufficient demarcation between fore-, middle- and background. He has, however, used the play of light on the bare earth and on the subject to good effect.

There is just a suggestion, in the backdrop of trees, that Gainsborough is already aware of the work of the French landscape artists, such as Watteau and Fragonard, whose work was at that time being introduced into the London art world by his teacher Hubert Gravelot and by the Rococo painter Jean-Baptiste van Loo.

Bumper, a Bull Terrier

Painted 1745
35.6 × 30.5 cm
Private Collection

Although elements of this picture may have been taken from sketches made by Gainsborough in Suffolk (it bears a strong resemblance to parts of the Suffolk coast), it is unlikely that it represents a topographical scene.

Comparison with the river landscape of 1774–5 (page 45) shows that Gainsborough's ability has developed at a tremendous pace. Whereas the earlier work is hesitant and derivative, this is a strikingly confident and polished performance. Although it is still basically Dutch in inspiration, there are clear signs both of Gainsborough's developing individuality and of the growing influence of French Rococo landscape art.

The curious emptiness of the scene, peopled only by distant figures and animals, was not without precedent in the Dutch tradition, particularly in the work of Ruisdael, the strongest single influence on Gainsborough's early landscape work. But the very animated picture surface was a lesson drawn from the French school. Apart from the more convincing perspective and sophisticated geometry of this work in comparison with the earlier river landscape, it is principally Gainsborough's ability to use light as a dramatic and unifying element which most clearly demonstrates his growing maturity. The concern for re-creating an atmosphere, over and above formal or narrative considerations, prefigures his later ability, in more sophisticated works such as *The Morning Walk* and the portrait of *Mrs Sheridan* (pages 131 and 121), to convey a strong atmospheric sense through his attention to the picture as a whole rather than as a collection of disparate elements.

A View in Suffolk

Painted c.1746–7
47 × 61 cm
National Gallery of Ireland, Dublin

Most scholars agree that this is a self-portrait with his fiancée or wife, Margaret Burr. Apart from the physical resemblance to himself, the thoroughly French Rococo style of the picture is thought to indicate that it was intended by Gainsborough as a light-hearted, celebratory, and above all personal work. It clearly demonstrates the young artist's facility with the French as well as the Dutch manner, though while this is a capable pastiche it does not come as close to the style of Watteau or Fragonard as does, for example, the river landscape (page 45) to Wijnants or *Cornard Wood* (page 53) to Ruisdael.

The stiff, doll-like figure of his wife derives no doubt from Gainsborough's habit of using small dolls as models, and although his own figure is slightly freer, it is by no means entirely satisfactory. What is remarkable, however, is his handling of Margaret's dress; at twenty-one he has managed to produce a finer painted description of fabric than many of his contemporaries achieved in a lifetime. The highlights on the satin overdress are painted with enormous confidence and skill, and there are already clear signs of the highly idiosyncratic and unconventional brushwork that he was to develop in his later large-scale pictures of fashionable society women. The highlighting of the wrinkle on Margaret's shoe and the tasselled fringe of the blue petticoat also have a degree of definition which is absent from the rest of the picture. The backdrop is just that – nothing more – so that one is encouraged to focus on the sitters. It is also evident that, despite occasional bravura touches, Gainsborough is not yet particularly competent with hands, as there are clear signs of heavy reworking.

Couple on a Bench
(Conversation in a Park)

Painted c.1746–7
76.2 × 67.3 cm
Musée du Louvre, Paris

In the last year of his life Gainsborough described this picture as 'a little in the schoolboy stile', and also recorded that it, or an earlier version, persuaded his father to send him to London to study art. He also mentions that it had been bought and sold several times in the intervening forty years, and that he himself had purchased it at one time for nineteen guineas. It stands in stark contrast both to the delicate French taste of his marriage portrait and to the airy animation of the Dublin *View in Suffolk* (page 49). Ruisdael is the main influence here, displayed in the subject matter – a heavy, dark wooded scene – and in the strong feeling of an enclosed space with only narrow, distant perspectives.

It is an ambitious picture, which uses perspective cleverly to lead the eye along two distinct vistas, the track and the stream. Gainsborough has paid much more attention to the minute details of the foreground than in either of the earlier landscapes reproduced here, but there are a number of elements, such as the sunlit bare earth and the spotlit animal on the high bank beneath the dark trees on the left, which are familiar from earlier works. Most striking, however, is his command of the figures which, despite some problems of scale between the woodcutter in the foreground and the walker on the track, are very competently executed. As they show no signs of having been posed by dolls, it is possible that they are copied more or less directly from Dutch landscape works.

This has proved to be one of Gainsborough's most enduringly popular works, perhaps because of its superficial resemblance to the work of Constable, which gives it a more 'English' resonance.

Gainsborough's Forest (Cornard Wood)

Painted c.1746–8
121.9 × 154.9 cm
The National Gallery, London

It was in this picture, one of the most famous images of eighteenth-century Britain, that Gainsborough first demonstrated that he was capable of quite breathtaking originality. Painted as a wedding portrait, it approaches its subject in a strikingly innovative way, placing the couple well to one side of the image and setting them in an apparently topographical landscape (while it was accepted practice to centre the subjects in a decorative Arcadian scene). Gainsborough reversed the design in *Heneage Lloyd and his Sister* (page 57), but never again used it as boldly in a marriage portrait – although even his more conventional marriage portraits, such as *The Morning Walk* (page 131), still depart significantly from the norm.

The use of dolls to model the poses of the couple is once again apparent, and although Mr Andrews's clothing is carefully described, the lack of attention to the structure of the body beneath is plainly evident. The pose of his wife copies that of his fiancée, Margaret Burr, in Gainsborough's own wedding picture. Despite their naïvety, the figures are full of character and entirely believeable – as Gainsborough's friend Philip Thicknesse remarked, they are 'perfectly like but stiffly painted'.

Placing the couple in naturalistic countryside, and allowing the scenery to marginalize them to such a degree was a daring stroke, and eminently successful in conveying a sense of their ease within their inherited rural domain. Though the picture is clearly unfinished – Mrs Andrews's dress shows none of the detail of Margaret's in the earlier work, and she was to have had a pheasant in her lap, and there are some distinct irregularities of space and perspective – the freshness and immediacy of the image and its lack of pretentiousness have ensured its continuing popularity and a central place in our perception of eighteenth-century Britain.

There has been some debate as to whether the landscape depicted is a real one – the Andrews' home

Mr and Mrs Andrews
Painted c.1748–50
69.8 × 119.4 cm
The National Gallery, London

was at Bulmer in Suffolk. Although the evidence is inconclusive, it seems likely that having determined to set his clients in realistic rather than mythological countryside, Gainsborough would indeed have chosen to show them in front of their own property.

The Lloyd family lived at Hintlesham Hall, Suffolk, but although this is the accepted title of the picture, the identity of the sitters is not absolutely certain. Gainsborough has here used the same pictorial device – albeit reversed – as he did in *Mr and Mrs Andrews* (page 55), although the effect is less striking because of the different shape of the canvas, the more obviously contrived setting and the closeness of the subjects to the picture plane. He has also used a much more sombre palette, in which blue and yellow tones are almost entirely absent. Once again there are signs that the picture is unfinished – the ghostly hemline below the girl's dress, for instance – and there are several points where the artist's lack of confidence with scale and perspective are apparent. For example, the mirror-like surface of the lake is too foreshortened to make the mature tree behind it square with our perception of the small tree growing in front of the balustrade, although the tree on the left is perfectly to scale with the ruined church beyond. The lake itself looks suspiciously like a piece of glass or a mirror, which is probably exactly what it was, for Gainsborough composed his landscapes on a small table in his parlour, using bits of mirror, coal and sticks, and even broccoli for the trees. Another curious oversight is that the stone post of the balustrade, which occupies the central foreground, is several degrees out of true, thus making Miss Lloyd look as though she is leaning more than she is.

Nevertheless, the image is a delightful one, depicting the children in an Arcadian setting which is at once both civilized (the classical architecture) and mysterious, even vaguely threatening (the girl holds an arrow and the boy a bow). Gainsborough has managed to convey vividly their expressions despite their physical awkwardness and has done his best to disguise an error in the drawing of Heneage Lloyd's right arm by colouring it more darkly than the rest of his jacket.

This is an ambitious work and perhaps shows that Gainsborough was attempting to work in a genre

Heneage Lloyd and his Sister

Painted c.1751–2
64.1 × 80 cm
The Fitzwilliam Museum, Cambridge

with which he was not very familiar. Most of his clients at this time were middle class, for whom this kind of setting would have been pretentious and unsuitable, but the Lloyds seem to have demanded something altogether more rarified than ordinary fields and hedges. Gainsborough responded with typical inventiveness with this intuitively rather than studiedly classicized setting, though he must by this time have seen enough French art, at least in engravings, to give him a clear idea of the style required.

Gainsborough borrowed the pose for Mr Plampin from an engraving after a painting by Watteau *Antoine de la Roque* (see page 15), and, to judge from the engraving, Mr Plampin appears a good deal more comfortably seated than his bucolic French counterpart. It is the sort of composition – modest though it is – that Gainsborough must have relished during his Suffolk years, when the vast majority of his sitters demanded only a simple waist- or shoulder-length likeness against a plain dark background.

There are signs here that Gainsborough is managing to overcome the problem of the stiff-limbed attitudes conditioned by his use of mannequins, though there is still some awkwardness. He has learnt, for example, that if he wrinkles the cloth of the sitter's stockings, his calves look much less tubular than if he leaves them smooth. And, although the tree is sketchily done, a considerable amount of time has been spent on the fancy, braided waistcoat and jacket, the detail picked out in the slanting late afternoon light, giving the whole picture its warm, calm tone.

The distant landscape is strongly reminiscent of, though less finished than that in *Mr and Mrs Andrews* (page 55). The picture's chief oddity is the dog, who gazes rather longingly at his master's glove rather than his face as was presumably intended, and whose legs mimic those of his master rather too closely for the geometry of the picture to bear. In fact, the dog's pose seems to be derived from Mr and Mrs Andrews' pet (Gainsborough may have used the same sketch), albeit with one hind leg strangely awry.

John Plampin

Painted c.1753–5
50.2 × 60.3 cm
The National Gallery, London

This work is typical of a number of coastal scenes that Gainsborough painted during his Suffolk years, and although the scenery is imagined, it does bear a resemblance to the steep estuarine landscapes of East Anglia. Its chief interest lies in its very daring use of highlighting to suggest the evening sunlight. Gainsborough, of course, used this device often, but rarely pared it down so severely. In a particularly clever touch he has suggested the sun shining on the walls of the church; patches of brightness can just be glimpsed through the trees on the right, near the tiny cottage. Apart from the eye-catching church tower, the eye is led along a line of highlights and through the central horizontal line of the picture down the coast to two minute white sails on the horizon.

As is frequently the case in Gainsborough's early work, the masses of cloud and trees mirror the arrangement of the figures. Despite the artificiality of this device, it is the group of figures and animals which are, to our eyes, the more obviously contrived element of the work; the landscape seems quite naturalistic in comparison with that of other early scenes such as the Edgehill landscape (page 45). The grouping of figures and beasts, and the peasant costumes, are still thoroughly Dutch in derivation, but there are typically personal touches of sharp observation: the receding couple with the cart just below the sandy bank, the sheepdog creeping around the groups of figures, the man asleep near the cart, and the trunk of the silver birch tree. Despite its apparent simplicity, this is a complex and ambitious little work, executed with great care. Its dark tone may be an indication of Gainsborough's preoccupation with the work of Ruisdael, an influence which persists long after he has taken to producing more ornate, French-influenced landscapes.

Coastal Scene with Country Cart (View near the Coast)

Painted c.1750–5
81.2 × 107.7 cm
Ipswich Borough Council Museums & Galleries

Although there are strong similarities between this landscape and the earlier Edgehill and Dublin paintings (pages 45 and 49), we can once again detect clear advances in Gainsborough's technique. The construction of the picture is particularly close to the *View of Suffolk*, but the highly animated surface of that work has given way to a smoother, calmer and more limpid scene. In fact, the arrangement of the topography and figures is a return to a more direct revision of Dutch painting and, compositionally, is Gainsborough's most competent performance to date. The main features are essentially the same: the sunlit bank, framing tree, and the small, dark tree forming the focus of the composition just left of centre. But the effect here is very different, suggesting rustic contentment rather than the somewhat unsettling loneliness of the Dublin landscape.

Once again, Gainsborough seems to have managed the figures rather more convincingly than in his portraits and, as in *Cornard Wood* (page 53), they may have been derived from sketches made from Dutch paintings. The presence of figures in his landscapes becomes considerably more pronounced from now on, increasingly providing an anecdotal focus, often of courtship, as is here implied by the couple on the left. Only the distant figure on the track seems awkward and superfluous. The dog on the jetty, barking at the bird swooping over the water, is a brilliant touch, animating the otherwise thoroughly conventional and static right-hand half of the image.

But it is the use of light which is perhaps the most telling feature of the work, in that for once Gainsborough has curbed his instinctive reliance on contrasting brilliant highlights and gloomy shadows, in favour of allowing the light to fall in broader, softer swathes, and considerably reducing his reliance on strongly 'spotlit' foreground detail. By shifting the focus to the pale track beyond the brown cow and the bank above it, he pulls our gaze deep into the picture,

Extensive River Landscape with View of Cornard Village

Painted c.1753
76.2 × 151.1 cm
National Gallery of Scotland, Edinburgh

marginalizing the couple in the foreground and forcing us to seek them out. We thus read the picture as a whole rather than focusing on a particular passage, and the entire landscape becomes the subject rather than just the background of the picture.

Bought by the Duke of Bedford from Gainsborough on 24 May 1755 for twenty-one guineas, this sizeable landscape is typical of the kind of sentiment that public taste demanded in English landscape painting. Landscapes at this time were considered a decorative rather than a fine art, and scenes such as this hung in the drawing rooms of scores of country houses less grand than Woburn Abbey. What Gainsborough achieved in the two decades after this picture was painted was the re-invention of the landscape tradition. He succeeded in bringing the genre to the forefront of public and critical attention by retaining the anecdotal scenes of rustic life, but placing them within a wholly new type of landscape that was an amalgam of Dutch and Baroque elements, with the emphasis on the total design rather than on the anecdote, and on painterly qualities rather than strict verisimilitude.

The attention of the viewer is called directly to the couple in the foreground, as the background is a loose confection of almost haphazardly placed incidental detail. However, Gainsborough was not expecting this picture to be viewed in the way that, say, the Edinburgh scene (page 63) was designed to be explored, as a total entity. He was producing a standard, old-fashioned painting for a client who wanted a particular sort of image on his wall. It cannot be denied that it is an uneven picture, with the thin, barely credible framing tree on the left in stark contrast to the superb handling of the stag-headed oak, and the awkward perspective of the fence running back towards the village at odds with the beautiful touch of white on the cap of the peasant woman on the hillock. The great oak was a feature which Gainsborough used on several occasions at around this time, just as the sand or bare chalk bank was a favourite device in his earlier work.

Woodcutter Courting a Milkmaid

Painted 1755
106.7 × 128.2 cm
By kind permission of the Marquess of Tavistock,
and the Trustees of the Bedford Estates

Alice Kirby was the mother of Gainsborough's closest friend Joshua Kirby, later President of the Society of Artists, and this is typical of the type of portrait that was Gainsborough's 'bread and butter' during his Suffolk years. In these pictures the subject is depicted in half-profile or facing the viewer, and is set in a *trompe l'oeil* oval surround against a plain, dark background. He produced scores of such pictures for a few guineas a time, a process which irked him considerably but which provided the best possible training for an aspiring portraitist.

This portrait, however, shows how this simple, almost austere formula could become in Gainsborough's hands the most striking purveyor not only of the sitter's likeness but of her character. There is nothing mystical about this process; it rested entirely on the artist's ability to depict a precise nuance of expression. And, crucially, on his willingness to do so, for the great majority of these portraits lack such subtle insights into character. Only in portraits of those he knew, whose faces were more familiar to him than the rapid succession of run-of-the-mill customers, however closely observed, do we see that he has been at pains to convey not merely a passing resemblance but a true likeness. The portrait is clearly the work of a more confident artist than the painter of Mr and Mrs Andrews and the Lloyd children, and it has been suggested that this places the work in the late 1750s – although John Kirby's picture was done in 1752 or 1753. But, as the picture of his daughters painted in 1755 clearly shows (page 69), Gainsborough was capable – given the motivation – of this kind of well-modelled and vivid work by the middle of the decade. Stylistically, on the evidence of that picture, there is no reason to suppose that Mrs Kirby's barely concealed amusement and gimlet stare were set down any later than 1755.

Mrs John Kirby (née Alice Brown)

Painted c.1755
75.8 × 62.9 cm
The Fitzwilliam Museum, Cambridge

Gainsborough's daughters were about four and six years old when he painted this picture, one of several double and single portraits he made of them over the years. They were affectionately known in the family as 'Molly and The Captain'.

This charming portrait shows clear evidence of Gainsborough's ability to portray the human figure in a vivid and immediate way by the middle of the 1750s. The stiffness and formality of his earlier portraits has here entirely vanished, yet curiously is still to be seen in many of his works over the next few years. The reason for this must lie in his continuing reliance on mannequins to pose his commissioned portraits, but the question remains as to why he persisted with this practice if he was able to produce so much more lifelike results without it. The answer must firstly be that as the use of dolls was so widespread at the time, the rather wooden look of his figures would have been far less noticeable to him and his public; this was simply how many portraits looked. Secondly, of course, Gainsborough was able to spend much more time with his children than with his clients, and indeed all the indications are that he preferred to detain his sitters for as short a time as possible – just long enough to get the face right. Thirdly, as with *Mrs Kirby* (page 67), we can surmise that this was partly a question of motivation; Gainsborough was not one to expend more effort on a picture than was necessary to satisfy a client, and only with portraits of those to whom he was close did he take extraordinary pains, as is obvious here despite the unfinished state of the picture.

The poses, as well as the beautiful modelling of the faces, are a great advance on his earlier portrait work. The children appear to be about to pass on either side of the viewer, as Margaret turns away after the butterfly, giving a 'snapshot' effect unusual in pictures of children at that date, when the kind of stiff repose seen in *Heneage Lloyd and his Sister* (page 57) was the standard treatment.

The Painter's Daughters chasing a Butterfly

Painted c.1755–6
113.7 × 104.8 cm
The National Gallery, London

Richard Canning was the rector of Hawkstead, Suffolk and a former curate of St Lawrence's, Ipswich. He was a close friend of John and Joshua Kirby, who probably obtained the commission for Gainsborough. This striking portrait of the minister marks an experimental phrase in Gainsborough's portrait technique, for while the format is the traditional one he used in *Mrs Kirby* (page 67) and scores of others, the modelling of the face has been achieved by a system of very exact, minute hatched brushstrokes, quite different from his usual broad and dynamic approach. The result when seen from the appropriate distance (or if you half-close your eyes) is an almost uncannily realistic image. Although Gainsborough adapted this system in later work he never used it so precisely again, so it would appear that he found it unsatisfactory despite the superb results. Very probably it was too time-consuming; he may also have decided that it concealed too well the hand of the artist, for he was determined that his great technical facility should be visible and appreciated.

It needs to be stressed that this degree of realism was unusual in portraiture at the time, and would have appeared strange to contemporary eyes – though it was perhaps more acceptable in portraits of ordinary country people such as the Reverend Canning and Mrs Kirby than it would have been in the sort of image typified by *John Plampin* (page 59). Society folk, whether urban or from the squirearchy, expected to be flattered by a smooth, oval-faced depiction, and this demand for conformity remained a visible influence in Gainsborough's work for some time. Credit must be given to artists such as Ramsay, and in particular Reynolds, for introducing into grand portraiture a more fully modelled style derived from Italian art; Hogarth did not flatter his clients either, but in the 1750s the example of painters such as Devis, Hudson and Gainsborough's teacher Hayman was still widely followed.

The Reverend Richard Canning

Painted 1757
76.2 × 63.5 cm
Ipswich Borough Council Museums & Galleries

Gainsborough probably met the Kilderbees soon after moving from Sudbury to Ipswich in about 1750, and they remained close friends for the rest of his life. He painted Samuel more than once, but this is his only picture of Mary. Its format is typical of the half-lengths of the Ipswich period, with the painted oval surround and plain background; the pose, too, is very similar to a number of near-contemporary works. He has, however, lavished special attention on the dress, even altering it a few years later to bring it into line with current fashions. The modelling of the face is smooth, with none of the brushiness of his picture of the Reverend Canning (plate 71), and he has echoed the ripple of lace on the dress with a flowing lock of hair over her left shoulder.

The Kilderbees were very helpful in seeking out potential clients for the struggling young painter. Legend has it that a local farmer, prompted by Samuel, once asked Gainsborough to go out and see him, which he did, only to discover that he was expected to paint the man's fence instead of his portrait. It is possible that Gainsborough took the job; he was charging only eight guineas a head at the time and he is known to have helped out another friend, Joshua Kirby, with his carriage and signpainting work. Mrs Kilderbee would have paid fifteen guineas for this picture; had she been in London and gone to sit for the young Reynolds she would have been charged twice this amount. Even so, Gainsborough's prices were by no means cheap for the time. A guinea (twenty-one shillings) represented several weeks' wages for an agricultural worker, and Gainsborough's rent for a year in a fashionable house at Bath was only 50 pounds, or three half-length portraits. But at Ipswich work was not easy to come by, and he may have been grateful for extra income between commissions.

Mrs Samuel Kilderbee
(née Mary Wayth)

Begun 1757
73 × 60 cm
Ipswich Borough Council Museums & Galleries

Although in a less complete state than the picture of his daughters chasing a butterfly (page 69), with no part of the painting finished, this work shows Gainsborough once again using the opportunity afforded by an uncommissioned work to experiment with both pose and technique. The smooth finish of the earlier work has here been replaced, at least in the underpainting, by a system of short, animated strokes which build up the roundness of the girls' faces. It is not clear whether Gainsborough intended to leave the cat in the picture, as he has indicated the position of Margaret's arm, even where it would have been hidden by the animal, more strongly than the cat itself. The picture has been described as 'The Painter's Daughters Teasing a Cat', but this does not seem right. Mary, the older girl, is holding something in her right hand which may be a brush.

Gainsborough's pictures of his children – there exists a drawing of a sleeping baby which may be of one of them, as well as several other paintings in various stages of completion – are considerably more naturalistic than the efforts of many earlier eighteenth-century British painters. Children, particularly when shown in a family group, were very often depicted in a conventionalized and artificial way, with their doll-like, rosy faces indicating their glowing health and therefore their parents' conscientiousness and good fortune. This, like the demand for the smooth-faced, straight-limbed portraiture of adults, gradually went out of fashion in the 1750s and 1760s, and was supplanted by more thoroughly animated depictions. Lawrence's *Mrs Henry Baring and her Children* (see page 34), for example, despite its highly contrived construction, is far more vivacious than the family groups of Arthur Devis or than Hogarth's early work; Gainsborough's *Byam Family* (page 85) marks something of an intermediate point in the process of change.

The Painter's Daughters with a Cat

Painted c.1758–60
75.6 × 62.9 cm
The National Gallery, London

This was the first picture that Gainsborough executed after his move from Ipswich to Bath in 1759, and it was completed the following year. Ann Ford was the fiancée of Gainsborough's close friend and champion Philip Thicknesse. She was a brilliant musician who gave public recitals on both the viol da Gamba (a cello-like instrument) and the guitar.

Many writers have maintained that this portrait marks a revolution in Gainsborough's work, but although it was by far the grandest and most ornate he had produced so far, its execution does not in fact contain any painterly technique which cannot be found in earlier works. What is completely unprecedented is the exuberance and daring of the composition, which combines Baroque sinuousness with the majestic influence of Van Dyck; Gainsborough's sketches for this work are based on the Dutchman's portrait of *Lady Digby*. As was often the case, Gainsborough has reserved his finest and most painstaking work for a portrait of a friend. It is apparent as early as 1746 or 1747 that he was capable of brilliant drapery work, but the sheer complexity of Miss Ford's dress must nevertheless have posed an enormous challenge. In later efforts his nephew Gainsborough Dupont would help with this kind of work, but this was undoubtedly all by Gainsborough's own hand, at this time an unusual practice as most painters delegated to assistants or sent their pictures out to be finished by 'drapery men'.

Gainsborough has also learnt from Van Dyck the trick of distorting the body and has elongated the legs, not just to flatter the subject but to counteract the foreshortening effect of being viewed from below. The picture caused a great stir, but was not universally acclaimed, being thought by some, perhaps, to be overly 'showy'.

Mrs Philip Thicknesse

Painted 1759–60
197.1 × 135 cm
Cincinnati Art Museum, Ohio

John Hayes, in his notes for the catalogue of the Tate Gallery Gainsborough retrospective in 1980, suggests that this picture shows signs, in its concentration on the head and in particular the hands, that Gainsborough had been closely studying the recent work of his great rival Reynolds, who was rapidly becoming the country's most famous and highly paid artist. Hayes also points out that it was probably Gainsborough's habit of working by candlelight or lamplight in a darkened room which accounts for the difference in the play of light on the hands, which were closer to the source, and on the face, which being further away is more softly delineated. In normal conditions, by daylight, this effect would have been impossible. When painting, Gainsborough liked to stand at exactly the same distance from the canvas as the sitter was from himself – using brushes with very long handles – and this may account for the odd elongation of the arms, which have not been foreshortened to compensate for the distortion of the two-dimensional surface. This might also be the reason why Gainsborough added the chair after finishing the figure (preliminary drawings show a different one), in order to make sense of the problematic right arm.

In its modelling and tone the picture strongly resembles the much smaller and simpler portrait of the *Reverend Richard Canning* of three years earlier (page 71). Once again, we have the impression of great verisimilitude; the viewer is convinced in a way not encouraged by, for instance, the portrait of *General Johnston* (page 83) that this is exactly how the septuagenarian Mr Price looked. Incidentally, the drawing on the wall is an existing work by Gainsborough, not an invention for the portrait.

Uvedale Tomkins Price

Painted c.1760
124.1 × 99.1 cm
Staatsgemäldesammlungen, Munich

Although the spectacular changes that occurred periodically in Gainsborough's portrait style are often remarked upon, during the late 1750s and early 1760s his landscape art underwent a no less radical, though more subtle and gradual development. A comparison between this work and, for instance, the Ipswich *View near the Coast* or the *Woodcutter Courting a Milkmaid* at Woburn (pages 61 and 65) indicates just how fundamental these changes were. Both the earlier works may be summarized as setting out a formulaic landscape in which our attention is drawn to the central anecdotal subject by means of discrete highlights; although our eyes may roam around the rest of the scene, it is the narrative anecdote which demands our attention. Here, however, everything has been contrived to prevent our eyes resting on any particular passage. The subject of the picture has shifted away from a particular incident to the landscape itself – in the sense of both the scene itself and the way it is painted. In geographical terms, so to speak, we have left the quasi-East Anglian farmlands and entered a more mysterious and Romantic domain, an Arcadian and not entirely civilized realm. Gainsborough derived this type of landscape from the 'classicized' pastoral landscapes of Claude and Poussin. In construction, however, the work is thoroughly and exuberantly Baroque, a system of great curving lines and surfaces leading the eye inwards in a spiral towards the distant mountain. Only the heavy, dark trees still bear testimony to the Dutch influence on his art.

It is, however, the insistence with which Gainsborough directs our attention to his handling of paint which is the greatest departure from his earlier scenes. The picture is an astonishing technical achievement: the pin-sharp rendition of close detail in places resembles mezzotint or steel engraving, with a most elaborate fine highlighting on the stream in the foreground and on the twin dead trees in the left-hand middle ground. The superb sky, on the other hand, resembles a watercolour in its subtlety and complexity.

A Grand Landscape

Painted c.1763
141.6 × 157.5 cm
Worcester Art Museum, Massachusetts

That the portrait of Ann Ford does not represent a thorough revolution in Gainsborough's art is amply demonstrated by this engaging portrait of a dashing military figure; for though Gainsborough was never as daring in his male portraits as in his female ones, there are not many elements in this picture that depart from the full-lengths of the Suffolk period beyond the more dynamic pose and a greater attention to the overall geometry of the picture. There is still a suggestion of woodenness about the figure that contrasts sharply with the new style of heroic portraiture created by Reynolds and exemplified by his *Colonel John Hayes St Leger* (see page 27), in which the subject is shown on the battlefield, in a pose derived from the Apollo Belvedere. Gainsborough was quite possibly deliberately trying to avoid this new trend; his solution being to show the General leaning nonchalantly against a tree, but placing the legs so as to suggest that he is a man of action who might at any moment stride away. Compositionally, this is a quite brilliant solution, using as it does the tree trunk to continue the long curves of the General's legs and coat, but the pose is certainly more stilted than Reynolds's work of the same period.

Johnston's portrait is also unusual in the way that the figure fills the canvas from top to bottom. This may be another response to the problems posed by hanging the work at a considerable height; the re-laxed pose would be counteracted by exaggerating the domineering relationship of the figure to the viewer.

General James Johnston

Painted c.1763–4
206 × 141 cm
National Gallery of Ireland, Dublin

Gainsborough was always ready to adapt his portrait style to the needs of his clients, as the very traditional format of this picture shows. The promenade was a conventional device, but Gainsborough has enlivened it firstly by showing off his brilliant drapery technique and secondly by setting it within an unusually wild and dramatically handled landscape. The couple look as though they would be more at home on the lawn of a country house, which is where, in the work of most of Gainsborough's contemporaries, we would have found them. Another personal touch was to paint the child gazing frankly out at the viewer (or at the artist), which lends the whole image an immediacy it might otherwise have lacked.

The picture marks a midway point between the conventionality of an early work such as *John Plampin* (page 59), whose smooth features and slightly wooden posture are still discernible in Mr Byam, and the brilliant originality of *The Morning Walk* (page 131), in which the promenade format has been turned into a *tour de force* of rhythm and colour.

That Gainsborough still regarded portrait and landscape as separate exercises is clearly seen from the area of flat paint around and above Mrs Byam's head. Having, it seems, worked on the landscape background, leaving space for the figure (surely posed as usual by a doll), he then quickly filled in the gap once the figure was satisfactorily in place. It may even be that he painted in the dress up to the neckline and filled in the portrait head afterwards. Artists very often had studio props of ornate antique costumes to suit the wishes of their various clients, such dress being the fashion in portraiture. It was only later in his career that Gainsborough seems to have hit upon the idea of unifying his canvases by basing his background landscapes on the rhythms and colours of his sitters' dress – a technique seen at its best in *Mrs Richard Brinsley Sheridan (page 121)*.

The Byam Family

Painted c.1764
248.9 × 238.8 cm
Marlborough College, Wiltshire

Although not as complex or as ambitious as the extraordinary Worcester *Grand Landscape* (page 81), we see here how Gainsborough was able to re-invent the very traditional form of anecdotal landscape typified by the Woburn *Woodcutter Courting a Milkmaid* (page 65) by setting it within a more thoroughly Romantic domain. The broad classicism of the Worcester pastoral has given way to a small, secret dell in which the boy can court the milkmaid as his cart lumbers along the lane. In sentiment, and in its setting in an enclosed woodland space rather than an open pastoral one, this is much closer to the French School and in particular to the work of Jean-Honoré Fragonard (1732–1806), whose best known work *The Swing* is exactly contemporary; though perhaps a more likely influence would have been Jean Antoine Watteau (1684–1721) – like Gainsborough an admirer of Rubens – whose work was widely available in engravings and from which Gainsborough borrowed directly on occasion. From this point onwards Gainsborough's landscape work increasingly falls within the two categories of broad pastoral vistas and thickly wooded enclosed intimate scenes such as this one.

Once again the use of a single, low light source pared down to an absolute minimum of highlighting lends the picture greater dramatic force, adding to the impression that the viewer is 'spying' on an intimate moment unknown to the couple (or the dog, who is clearly worried about getting home).

This type of sentimental landscape rapidly became popular during the 1760s and 1770s, being considered a 'high' art form rather more readily in public opinion than the more humdrum type of landscape from which it is derived – the *Coastal Scene with Country Cart*, for example (page 61). This was because in accentuating the narrative role the painter was claiming a level of invention more comparable to that of the poet, then afforded the highest cultural status, than to the journeyman-painter of country houses and topographical views. This increasing 'literariness' continued to be a feature of academic

Wooded Landscape with Country Waggon, Milkmaid and Drover

Painted 1766
144 × 119.4 cm
Private Collection

landscape painting for decades afterwards, culminating in the strongly narrative work of some of the Pre-Raphaelites such as Sir John Everett Millais and William Holman Hunt. Figures no longer merely decorate a landscape; the landscape accentuates and amplifies the narrative generated by the figures, as if the picture were an illustration of a scene from a poem or novel – which in Victorian times, of course, it often was. Gainsborough refined this kind of picture considerably between 1764 and his death, and developed his 'fancy pictures' – sentimental images such as *The Cottage Girl* (page 127) – as a way of bringing the narrative subject to the fore, the landscape itself becoming as secondary as in his portrait work.

The grouping of the figures in and around the waggon is derived – though not directly – from Rubens's *Descent from the Cross* in Antwerp Cathedral. Gainsborough would have known the work from an engraving and also from one of Rubens's preliminary studies, which was at Corsham Court, Wiltshire at this date, and which Gainsborough copied. Prior to this work, Gainsborough had always subordinated the figures in his landscapes to the scenery, so the picture marks a radical departure for him. Not until the *Cottage Door* series was he to attempt anything like such a complex arrangement of figures again.

Although the positions of the figures are melodramatic, their postures implying unnecessary exertion, the picture is otherwise superbly constructed, beautifully balanced within an egg-shaped area in the lower two-thirds of the canvas. The eye is immediately drawn to the violent diagonal of the men with the bottle and the girl climbing up the wheel, and this line leads on into the trees behind, which are painted with particular flamboyance. The carthorse with the drooping head is common to many of Gainsborough's pictures – compare, for example, the *Wooded Landscape with Country Waggon, Milkmaid and Drover* (page 87) – but whereas we might expect him to enliven the vista beyond with landscape features, Gainsborough has instead chosen to fill this compositional gap with a brilliant study of a youth trying to calm the leading horse. This animal is strikingly reminiscent of the work of Stubbs, a copy of whose great treatise *The Anatomy of the Horse* Gainsborough possessed.

The picture is enlivened by several other fine details, such as the straw, the cloth and the rake protruding from the floor of the cart, the fallen tree trunk that balances the curve of the track, and the wonderful play of dappled light over the standing figures. Gainsborough's daughter Mary is the seated figure looking up at the drinkers; Margaret is the girl being helped aboard.

The Harvest Waggon

Painted 1767
120.5 × 144.7 cm
The Barber Institute of Fine Arts, Birmingham

Gainsborough hated the fact that people admired his portraits over his landscapes, and would remove the latter from the studio, showing them only to people whom he knew would understand and appreciate them. He was a realist when it came to financial necessity, however, and it was with portraits such as this one that he secured his reputation as the only serious rival to Reynolds. *John Campbell, Duke of Argyll* is his most magnificent male portrait, a deliberate essay in splendour and grandeur. Against a remarkably restrained background, which barely hints at the usual Arcadian scene with classical ruins, Gainsborough presents his subject almost foursquare, apparently bracing himself under the sheer weight of his robes, his feet spread to maintain his balance. Gainsborough would probably not have considered setting his subject in the more informal kind of scenery that featured in *General Johnston* of a few years before (page 83) and, as with the slightly later *Mary, Duchess of Montagu* (page 93), has considerably sharpened his brushwork to render the fabrics and furs in extreme detail. (When he later chose to portray the Duke of Buccleuch leaning informally on a country embankment, he was attacked for inappropriate informality). The result, as with the very elegant *The Hon. Mrs Graham* (page 107) of a decade later, is a certain coldness and lack of empathy – no doubt deliberate – which emphasizes the subject's elevated social rank. Yet, as with the much more sympathetic portrait of the Duchess of Montagu, we are left with a vivid impression of the subject's personality; it is the face, in the end, which is most memorable, rather than the trappings.

John Campbell, 4th Duke of Argyll

Painted c.1768
235 × 154 cm
Scottish National Portrait Gallery, Edinburgh

As he had first shown with his remarkable portrait of *Mrs John Kirby* (page 67), Gainsborough was as good, if not better, a portrayer of older woman as of the pretty society girls who made his reputation. For all its complex trappings, this is in essence just as simple a picture as that of the plainly dressed Mrs Kirby, for in both Gainsborough has managed to capture a subtlety of expression so acutely that it is the face above everything which remains in our minds. Mrs Kirby seemed to be suppressing a smile; Mary Montagu exudes propriety and dignity but her face is also faintly softened by humour, so that what appears at first to be a stern expression becomes on closer examination a wise and serene one. The eye is led via one of Gainsborough's most sumptuous essays in drapery work down the arm to the hands, which are almost as powerful a focus as the face itself. Relaxed and wonderfully observed, they enormously enhance the atmosphere of calm and considered poise, while the rose is a masterful addition to the picture, completely altering what might otherwise seem an image of loneliness and sterility. The picture warrants long and detailed attention for it is full of magnificently drawn detail – the earring, the stunningly delicate lace (not merely suggested, as he came to do so often, but minutely depicted), and the exquisite colour and texture of the green silk dress.

Mary, Duchess of Montagu

Painted c.1768
125.7 × 100.3 cm
By kind permission of the Duke of Buccleuch and Queensberry

The circumstances under which Gainsborough accepted and produced this topographical commission (from a Mr Lane) are unknown. Only about half a dozen pictures of 'real' landscapes by him survive, and most of these are very early works. None of them resemble this in the least; nor do any of his imagined works. It is in some ways reminiscent of Dutch work, particularly the central motif of the cattle coming down to drink, but it does not really bear comparison with that tradition either; although both Ruisdael and Hobbema, two of his early heroes, favoured heavily wooded scenes, they were quite unlike that depicted here.

In fact, although at first glance this is the most 'naturalistic' landscape Gainsborough had produced for many years, it is deeply conventional and contrived in its composition, with the chief vertical axis given by the tree nearest the cattle, and triangular framing elements on either side, though these are multiplied – the punt pole and the leaning tree on the far bank, and the leaning trunks on the right. But the composition is thrown off balance because this right-hand axis is echoed so many times, in the three tree trunks and the standing figure in the boat. On the other hand, the colouring of the picture is superb.

In many ways the work is more reminiscent of Constable's naturalistic landscapes than those of the Dutch School, but this is perhaps inevitable given the subject, and although Constable professed great admiration for Gainsborough's work, their mature oeuvres have surprisingly little in common.

View near King's Bromley on Trent

Painted c.1768–71
117.5 × 168.3 cm
Philadelphia Museum of Art

This is arguably Gainsborough's finest male portrait, because although it has none of the grandeur and complexity of a work like *John Campbell* (page 91), it is far more original and engaging. Jonathan Buttall's father was an ironmonger in Soho and a friend of Gainsborough, but whether it was a commission is not known; Gainsborough frequently gave away paintings to his friends or exchanged them for other goods – to the despair of his wife. After being sold by the Buttall family early in the 1800s, the painting was owned by Gainsborough's great rival John Hoppner (1758–1810). It was exhibited at the Royal Academy in 1770 and caused a sensation, being compared favourably with its chief influence, the work of Sir Anthony Van Dyck.

If it was a commission, Gainsborough has taken the opportunity afforded by an indulgent patron, as with *Ann Ford, Mrs Philip Thicknesse* (page 77), completely to ignore convention and produce an image which, while an homage to an Old Master, is nevertheless utterly personal, showing in a highly Romantic and heroic pose an ordinary middle-class boy, in much the same way as Hogarth broke with convention in portraying his patron Captain Coram in 1740 (see page 12). Gainsborough later used the costume again in a portrait of Paul Cobb Methuen, but in a much more conventional format.

Although the central subject is arresting, the picture's effect is amplified considerably by the very loosely painted landscape and sky beyond. The repeated highlit creases in the jacket and breeches are set off against a background in which the trees and clouds are also constructed of short, angled strokes. Gainsborough has also implied a strong moon shining behind the boy's shoulders in order to match the lightest part of the costume with an echo of pale cloud. The sun is setting, or has set, on the low horizon, but Gainsborough has quite blatantly added a third light source – presumably the lamp in his studio – giving a strong gleam to the boy's brow and refracting off the shiny cloth. Even the two small lilies

Jonathan Buttall ('The Blue Boy')

Painted c.1770
177.8 × 121.9 cm
The Huntington Art Collections, San Marino

in the right foreground are exactly placed to balance the composition, and are possibly a reference to Sir Peter Lely (or Lily), Van Dyck's successor as Principal Painter to the King and another great essayist in drapery painting.

Elizabeth (1754–92) and Mary (1758–87) were the talented daughters of musician and impressario Thomas Linley, who was among Gainsborough's closest friends in Bath. Once again, Gainsborough has pulled out all the stops in a portrait painted for a close friend, and the picture in many ways prefigures his approach – thirteen years later – to the portrait of Elizabeth (page 121) which marks the culmination of his most Romantic style of portraiture. We see here, as in *The Blue Boy* (page 97), how Gainsborough is increasingly concerned with bonding his sitters to their surroundings, so that the whole picture works to suggest and amplify a mood. Desmond Shawe-Taylor in his study of eighteenth-century portraiture, argues that this can be seen as an expression of the concept of female 'sensibility' explored slightly later (but against exactly the same social background) by Jane Austen and in the more intensely Romantic novels of Ann Radcliffe: 'Elizabeth becomes dreamy and contemplative, Mary sweet-tempered' in the presence of 'natural' benevolent scenery. Their spirituality and delicacy of feeling, which found expression in the musicianship indicated by the score and guitar, is echoed in the ethereal and delicate surroundings. Shawe-Taylor identifies the sisters with dryads or wood spirits, personifications of the landscape. While this interpretation would of course have been possible for any contemporary viewer, Gainsborough himself was chary of any such classical references and it may be that to extrapolate the subjects from the landscape is to put the cart before the horse.

What is most noticeable about his approach to the picture is that the kind of realism which produced the exact folds of the Blue Boy's clothes has given way to an extreme nervous energy, delicate without being timid, producing the extraordinary assortment of attenuated strokes, scratches and flicks to which Reynolds referred so admiringly in his *Discourse* on Gainsborough. At close quarters those marks make no sense but at the correct distance they suddenly become visual forms. Look, for instance, at the wisps

The Linley Sisters
(Mrs Sheridan and Mrs Tickell)

Painted c.1772
199 × 153.1 cm
Dulwich Picture Gallery, London

which indicate that Mary is wearing a fine muslin shawl around her upper arms; seen close to, these might be odd growths sprouting from her dress, but at a distance the eye does all the work, filling in material which Gainsborough has not actually depicted at all.

The paint in places is extremely thin, sometimes almost scraped off, and it is difficult to tell which of the highlights are produced by scratching and which by flicks of white paint. Finally, we once again see how Gainsborough has used the direct gaze of one of the sitters, and the suggestion of her leaning slightly towards us, actively to engage us with the subject of the picture.

Gainsborough produced several pictures exploring the theme of the labourer returning to his large and contented family, the type of image which John Barrell identifies in *The Dark Side of Landscape* as an attempt 'to resist or deny the creation of [working-class] consciousness', to gloss the emerging social strife of the English countryside and reassure its landowners. Indeed, this picture was bought by the 4th Duke of Rutland in 1778. This should not be taken to mean that Gainsborough was deliberately producing political propaganda, but there can be no doubt that this type of imagery in art, as in the poetry of Gray or Goldsmith, was the cultural consequence of this social upheaval. What is being 'said' in the picture is that honest toil will reap the rewards of contentment, good health and plentiful food (note the boy eating). Furthermore, as Barrell points out, this kind of idyllic rural lifestyle is available only to the 'honest' country labourer, freed from all care and responsibility by the benevolence of his social superiors in return for his labour and his unquestioning devotion, whereas his masters have to contend with their responsibilities as the 'natural' guardians of the land and its inhabitants. It is, of course, by no means a literal transcription of rural England, but England, in the ideal conception of Gainsborough's Tory clients, is nevertheless what is directly signified.

Formally, the painting is a most interesting development of the sort of image of rural life typified by the *Wooded Landscape with Country Waggon, Milkmaid and Drover* (page 87); but for a change in occupation and an apparent polygamy, the family here might be a direct consequence of that assignation. The same low light source, darkened foreground and crescent-shaped perspective are all still present, but within that format much has changed. The dark, dense trees have given way to more schematic, decorative objects. The palette is far simpler and the brushwork much more intrusive. Most noticeable, however, is the replacement of the figures by a grouping which is, for all their peasant attire, firmly

Wooded Landscape with Family Group outside the Cottage ('The Woodcutter's Return')

Painted c.1772–3
146 × 120.6 cm
By kind permission of His Grace the Duke of Rutland

Italianate; the babies might be putti from some Renaissance ceiling. In fact, the Dutch-style peasants have given way to a 'classical' grouping of figures derived from the work of another Dutchman, Rubens, and the trees are also Rubensian. This was by far the most complex arrangement of figures Gainsborough had attempted since *The Harvest Waggon* (page 89), and its artificiality would have been at odds with his earlier, more naturalistic landscape style. Henceforth his landscape work is firmly in this 'poetic', sometimes almost fantastic mode, whether it represents flamboyantly Romantic upland scenery or, as here, the tranquillity of the rural idyll.

In an extraordinary contrast to the intimate land-scapes that had preoccupied him over the previous few years, Gainsborough has here produced a broad, uncluttered and misty landscape which combines the classical grandeur of Claude with the kind of imaginative mountain scenery (Gainsborough had not yet seen mountains) produced by Rubens. The first thing that should be noted about it is that it was one of the scenes which Gainsborough 'composed' from bric-a-brac on the 'little folding table' in his parlour – and it shows. This is not the Romanticized but still recognizable rural landscape of the Worcester scene or *The Woodcutter's Return* (pages 81 and 101), but a full-blown Arcadia, whose features parallel but are quite evidently different from 'natural' trees and mountains. The costume of the women is even nearer to classical dress than in *The Woodcutter's Return*.

As a composition, and particularly in its handling of light and shadow, it is remarkably bold. What appears at first glance to be a middle distance so shadowy as to be impenetrable proves, on closer inspection, to be a complex and very freely handled passage, full of subtle changes in tone and colour. Once again, one of Gainsborough's favourite devices is evident in the two figures on horseback beyond the valley, allowing us to make sense of the vast perspective and leading the eye out of the suggestive middle ground towards the sunlit town in the distance. It is, however, that distant horizon and the sky above it which constitute the most unexpected part of the picture, another of those occasions when – without any precedent even in his own art – Gainsborough produces a completely masterful addition to his repertoire. The dimly seen buildings and half-delineated mountain beyond, and the pearly obscurity of the evening air are in a completely different league from the vista in, for example, the Woburn *Woodcutter Courting a Milkmaid* (page 65), or the hard, rather cold distance of the Worcester scene. In its subtlety

A Mountain Valley with Rustic Figures, a Shepherd and Sheep, and a Distant Village and Mountains

Painted c.1773–7
122 × 149 cm
Yale Center for British Art, Paul Mellon Collection

and opalescence this background reminds us more strongly of the work of Turner – particularly his Italian landscapes – than of any artist contemporary with or preceding Gainsborough. It was an idea he was to use again, but rarely to such good effect.

This is among the best of Gainsborough's standard portraits, the type of picture that was his bread and butter and which, as he remarked, 'kept the Pot boiling'. By the mid-1770s he had found a grand portrait style which combined formality of pose with informality of setting, whilst remaining adaptable and requiring no great physical or imaginative effort. Although now badly in need of cleaning, this work demonstrates how Gainsborough continued to use the kind of landscape scenery he had chosen to surround *General Johnston* (page 83) as a simple and effective framing device for his subjects. It is, in fact, much the same system as he used in *The Linley Sisters* (page 99) and distantly derives from the more basic traditional device of the framing tree in *John Plampin* (page 59). But the kind of extreme abstraction appropriate to the delicate female sentiment of *The Linley Sisters* (or later to the portrait of *Mrs Brinsley Sheridan* – page 121) would have been entirely inappropriate to a man of the stature of Wilkinson. Most of Gainsborough's male portraits are handled in a drier, more matter-of-fact style than his women, and the depiction of details of dress, as well as the greater solidity of their surroundings, shows a more disinterested approach which occasionally topples over into carelessness and banality. Wilkinson's jacket, for example, is given only the most basic attention, though partly to show up the splendour of his fancy waistcoat and cravat; even the wrinkles on his hose are no more than cursorily indicated. But, as always, we are in no doubt as to its value as a portrait, as an expression of character. Mr Wilkinson's great physical presence is striking, and his faintly humorous gaze does not mask the suggestion of a certain toughness of character.

Hayes comments that Gainsborough's depiction hints at Wilkinson's unscrupulousness, but perhaps shrewdness would be a less sweeping charge.

John Wilkinson (1728–1808) was one of the great figures of the early Industrial Revolution, the founder of the iron-making dynasty which is dimly recalled today in the Wilkinson's Sword brand of razor blade.

John Wilkinson

Painted c.1775
234 × 145 cm
Staatliche Museen zu Berlin

The family began in business as makers of weapons, and were the chief suppliers of cannon to the British army.

John Hayes also points out that the distant landscape is distinctly Claudian in conception, which parallels the increasingly Claudian development of Gainsborough's 'pure' landscapes during the mid-1770s.

Gainsborough painted this formal full-length portrait, in which his technique in the format reaches its full maturity, at the height of his success as a society painter. His style has noticeably hardened once again in comparison to *The Linley Sisters* (page 99), suggesting that he still felt constrained in his pictures of clients – as opposed to those of friends – to produce a more conventional type of image. But, if it is conventional – and this is perhaps as close as Gainsborough ever gets to the work of Reynolds – it is by no means mundane.

Reynolds, while a competent painter of silks and satins, tended to dress his sitters in simple, classical dress, and though other leading artists such as Romney and Hamilton shared Gainsborough's fondness for glamorous costume, neither of them could match him in depicting it in paint. Not only does Gainsborough seem to have deliberately chosen the most complex arrangement of fabric but, further to infuriate his contemporaries, he paints it with a verve and energy which was quite beyond them. Perhaps as a result of this conspicuous display of his talents, Gainsborough was attacked for what was held to be overdone colouring, particularly his fondness for purple, which is very prominent here. No doubt the vividness of his colours derives in part from his habit of painting in subdued light, but he was also a great technical experimenter, and his use of multiple layers of translucent paint adds a great softness and depth of colour to his work. He had a naturally inquisitive mind and later experimented extensively with painting on glass, in common with his friend de Loutherburg.

Although Gainsborough did not flatter his sitters overtly, he was not above a little subtle exaggeration, and one suspects that Mrs Graham's fashionably swan-like neck is the result of artistic licence. Everything in the composition (designed to be seen with the base of the picture 7 or 8 feet from the ground) has been arranged to stress the vertical and thus emphasize the willowy grace of the subject. We are carefully directed to notice, by way of the impossible piece of

The Hon. Mrs Graham

Painted c.1775–7
237 × 154 cm
National Gallery of Scotland, Edinburgh

flummery under her left arm, that she is reclining against a pillar, despite her effortless poise. The pose is taken from his (very bad) portrait of *John Eld* of 1772. The overgrown classical columns indicate that she personifies the civilized nobility of the bygone classical age, yet she remains to the viewer proud, cold and aloof. For all its brilliance, it is not an engaging image, and there are no signs that Gainsborough felt any empathy with his subject.

In many ways 1777 was Gainsborough's *annus mirabilis*, when he produced several of his most glamorous portraits and one of his greatest landscapes, *The Watering Place*. Frances Duncombe (1757–1827), the daughter of the Earl of Radnor, had first sat for Gainsborough four years earlier; possibly this portrait was to celebrate her recent engagement. Gainsborough also painted her younger sister Ann in 1777, though in a much less grandoise style.

Despite the similarity of approach – the classical ruins, Arcadian landscape, Van Dyckian costume and the turn of the head – between this portrait and that of *The Hon. Mrs Thomas Graham* (page 107), the difference in atmosphere is striking. Where the latter is languid and perhaps even petulant, the former is energetic and cheerful, and though there can be no possible doubt as to her lofty social standing, Frances Duncombe's portrait is infinitely more engaging. In terms of the tone and colour of the backgrounds, the two are also very similar, but the dress Gainsborough has chosen for Miss Duncombe is of the same blue as Jonathan Buttall's costume, one of his favourite colours. The greys, pinks and purples of Mrs Graham's costume, which gives that picture a rather acid tone, are here replaced by warmer and darker ones, although the skin tone is noticeably paler.

The classical architecture, relegated to the background, would appear to be a temple, since behind the pillar a statue in a niche is suggested – presumably of Aphrodite. The presence of someone who can only be her lover is suggested by the smile of recogniton breaking on her face; her gaze, in contrast to Mrs Graham's, is clearly focused on something. And while the pillar upon which Mrs Graham leans has been brilliantly enlivened by the tendril that flickers across its base, the tree around which Miss Duncombe is walking defines the space between viewer and viewed much more satisfactorily, as Gainsborough has left its edges unfocused, exactly as it would be if we were looking at the woman in real space. As in *The Blue Boy* (page 97), Gainsborough has made no secret of

The Hon. Frances Duncombe

Painted c.1777
233.7 × 154.9 cm
The Frick Collection, New York

the artificiality of the light, with the sunset clearly visible behind and the chief source so bright and direct that it can only be lamplight. This feature is even more pronounced than in *Mrs Graham*. It is to *The Blue Boy* that we should also look for the earliest sign of the influence of Van Dyck, which Gainsborough brought to such a grand climax in these two portraits; that combination of formality and contemporary Romanticism which is as dominant a theme (though in a different form) in *John Wilkinson* (page 105) as it is here.

This is one of Gainsborough's most arresting intimate portraits, and one much discussed in relation to his personal life. There is no doubt that he and Margaret had at times a difficult relationship, though few commentators blame Gainsborough, despite his bouts of drunkenness, his quick temper, spendthrift ways and philandering. Instead, Margaret is largely seen as the guilty party, firstly for giving him syphilis, which was inherited by their children, for alienating him from his friends – in particular Philip Thicknesse – and not least for continually harrassing him over the family income and expenditure. Gainsborough's letters alternately praise his wife to the skies (as when she nursed him through his severe illness of 1753) or damn her with faint praise: 'my wife is weak but good and never much formed to humour my Happiness.'

Although there seems little doubt that they exasperated each other, their mutual love was strong, as evidenced by this picture. Hayes also calls it 'immensely sympathetic' and so it is, though the phrase perhaps implies a somewhat patronizing attitude on Gainsborough's part to a woman we know next to nothing about. Only Isabelle Worman, of all Gainsborough's biographers, comes to her defence.

The picture is a brilliant development of the type of oval-set portrait, as typified by *Mrs John Kirby* (page 67), which Gainsborough had produced in Suffolk. Whereas those earlier images are still and quiet, this one is full of life, catching the fleeting gesture of Margaret pushing back her hood to allow the light to shine on her face. The hood replaces the *trompe l'œil* oval surround and, in contrast to the sketchily suggested clothes of earlier sitters such as Mrs Kirby and Richard Canning (pages 67 and 71), the costume is depicted with enormous energy, heightening the impression of suspended movement.

The restless position of Margaret's hands, the suggestion of a tilt to the head, and her enquiring gaze as if listening to some remark being uttered by her husband all combine to provide us with what is undoubtedly one of Gainsborough's finest works. No

Mrs Gainsborough

Painted c.1778
76.6 × 63.8 cm
Courtauld Institute Galleries, London

one in the late eighteenth century but he could have got away with such a confident abstraction as the series of coarse ochre brushstrokes that defines her upper right sleeve; and no-one else could have recreated the appearance of black lace from such an apparently chaotic series of scumbles and scratches. That such an utterly frank, tantalizing image should be our only substantial connection with Margaret's evidently fascinating personality is indeed a tragedy.

This picture, exhibited at the Royal Academy Exhibition in 1780, when it was rapturously received, is one of a series of closely related images which includes *The Woodcutter's Return* (plate 101), a famous picture of 1778 now in Cincinnati *The Cottage Door with Children Playing*, and *The Cottage Door with Peasant Smoking* (page 137). In all of these the theme of the idyllic rustic home is explored in various ways, using similar compositional elements but a wide variety of atmospheric effects. In the Cincinnati picture the woodcutter is an almost exact reproduction of the figure in *The Woodcutter's Return*, but here this figure is absent, and this has the effect of changing the mood from one of calm to one of anxiety. This atmosphere is greatly enhanced by the marked agitation of the handling and the gloominess of the surrounding scenery. Whereas in *The Woodcutter's Return* the scene is bathed in golden light, and the figures at the door are as passive as marble statues, here the family is menaced by the father figure's absence in the face of the forces of Nature. The light is fitful, the sky noticeably more stormy than before, the trees apparently blasted by the wind. The dead tree, which corresponds to the one beside the cottage in the earlier picture, is here handled in Gainsborough's most aggressive manner, thus becoming a sinister rather than a homely feature. It interrupts the violent flow of brushstrokes radiating out from the tree across the stream into the centre of the canvas, so that the family is threatened rather than sheltered by their surroundings. Even the footbridge over the stream seems on the verge of collapse. The cottage is even meaner than that in the earlier picture and has become a refuge from, rather than a home within nature. Although the children are self-absorbed, their mother is distracted, and there is no sign of an approaching figure in the distance.

The arrangement of the figures is far less contrived than that in *The Woodcutter's Return*; the pyramidal solution used here switches the responsibility for the family to the mother, whose role as child-rearer –

The Cottage Door
Painted c.1780
147.3 × 119.4 cm
The Huntington Art Collections, San Marino

rather than the father's as provider – has become the subject of the picture. Her expectant gaze shows that she is anxious enough to ignore the demands of the baby who stares up at her face.

Gainsborough has used a noticeably colder palette including a number of deep blue-green tones, even near the light-source on the left; the warmest tones are reserved for the area around the home. In design this is among his most Rococo landscapes, with the spiral centred on the shadow beyond the cottage framed 'behind' the violent triangle that is created by the framing trees.

Gainsborough remarked of Fischer that he 'had no more sense than his hautboy', which instrument is seen here lying on the top of the piano. Both Gainsborough's daughters were in love with the musician; Gainsborough expected Margaret to become engaged to him, and was taken aback when Mary proved to be the object of his affection. The marriage, however, was short-lived and disastrous. Fischer and Gainsborough had known each other for some years, often playing together at musical parties. One wonders whether Gainsborough would have produced such a magnificent portrait if he had thoroughly disliked the man; possibly he liked him well enough even though he thought him a fool. Later, when it turned out that Fischer had lied about his finances, they fell out completely.

As it is, this is undoubtedly one of Gainsborough's finest male portraits; confident, brilliantly designed, and executed with care and enormous virtuosity. Unusually, he has chosen a standard eighteenth-century format, with the accoutrements of Fischer's profession displayed in a drapery-swathed interior. Gainsborough would have enjoyed painting the props as much as the figure, for he was an enthusiastic collector of instruments and these are depicted with scrupulous care, even down to the maker's name on the piano. The pose, with the eyes raised – the composer listening to his Muse – is one which Gainsborough also used in his half-length portrait of Philip de Loutherburg. The figure is relaxed and well-modelled, but appears slightly odd in reproduction because, as usual, Gainsborough has elongated the torso to compensate for the high position in which the picture would be hung. Throughout the picture the painting is crisp and direct, with little of the showy brushwork for which by 1780 he was renowned. Every detail from the chair leg to the ink bottle, the studs in the upholstery to the staves of the music score are picked out to perfection, as is the subtle expression on the subject's face.

The palette is also somewhat unusual for Gains-

Johann Christian Fischer

Painted 1780
228.6 × 150.5 cm
Royal Collection, St James's Palace.
© Her Majesty the Queen

borough, a limited but well-balanced range of warm reds and browns which centres on Fischer's velvet suit. With his characteristic technique of bringing the picture space out towards the viewer, Gainsborough has made the pile of manuscripts in the foreground appear to break the picture plane, and has left them slightly out of focus so that they appear naturally indistinct when one is looking 'beyond' them at the figure. Note, too, how the floor appears to slope down from the chair to Fischer's shoes, whereas the pile of papers is on the horizontal because when correctly hung it would be almost at the viewer's eye level.

This may be one of the two seascapes of which Sir Horace Walpole wrote 'one steps back for fear of being splashed', which Gainsborough showed at the 1781 Royal Academy Exhibition. If he was talking about this picture, it was evidently its enormous energy rather than any strict verisimilitude that he was referring to, as it is one of the most obviously contrived compositions that Gainsborough ever produced. With its very dark foreground and exceptionally brilliant highlights – the two brightest points on the white rock mimicking the two sails – leading on to the long lateral cloud, Gainsborough has compressed the energy of the picture into a small central oval space. By this device he may have meant to suggest the force of the sea entering the cove, which is thus schematically turned on its side. The colour is very much brighter than in any of his contemporary landscapes, and the brushwork is exceptionally free, though interestingly it is the landforms which are painted most loosely; the waves are comparatively restrained. Despite the broad handling of much of the picture there are passages in the foreground picked out with great finesse. The picture was originally paired with another, calmer scene; this was the traditional manner of showing seascapes.

Seashore with Fishermen

Painted c.1781–2
102.2 × 127.9 cm
National Gallery of Art, Washington DC

Just as Gainsborough explored the compositional possibilities of the 'Cottage Door' scene in several canvases, so this picture is a revision of *A Mountain Valley with Rustic Figures, a Shepherd and Sheep, and a Distant Village and Mountains* (page 103) of ten years before. It is even more apparent here that he was using his table-top modelling technique to design the view, and the brushwork is considerably looser, but the central compositional elements are the same except for the absence of foreground figures. The main axis of the picture runs here from high on the left, down the wooded rock into the valley (which runs more directly towards us than in earlier versions), and on to the weir at the bottom right-hand side. The distant village, sunlit in the evening haze, is almost a copy of the earlier work, while the two travellers have been moved to the right.

Gainsborough made a tour of the Lake District in 1783 with his old Ipswich friend Samuel Kilderbee; though it is possible that he had visited Snowdonia a couple of years earlier, this may have been the first occasion on which he had seen real mountains. 'I propose to mount all the Lakes at the next Exhibition, in the great stile', he wrote, but although he made a number of sketches and drawings, no full-sized paintings emerged, and oddly the experience seems to have left little mark on his rendition of mountain scenery. One possible reason is simply that pressure of work prevented him from producing these topographical scenes – though since he had often rejected topographical commissions, he may have been joking.

1783 was one of Gainsborough's greatest years when, after a comparatively quiet time following his move from Bath, he produced a flood of magnificent portraits and landscapes; only in 1777 and 1785 did he complete more undisputed masterpieces. Perhaps, also, he felt no need to revise what had become his trademark: the peculiar amalgam of Romantic and rustic scenery with which he had single-handedly revivified the genre in Britain. The choice of the Lakes is an interesting one; still regarded as terrifyingly

Rocky Landscape
Painted 1783
119.4 × 147.3 cm
National Gallery of Scotland, Edinburgh

remote and awe-inspiringly wild, they were just becoming fashionable as taste swung markedly in favour of the Romantic in literature and painting, and as the landscapes of the south which had inspired the celebration of more pastoral scenes were gradually changing under the new mechanization in agriculture.

Gainsborough's approach to this painting leaves no doubt that it was intended as a showpiece as much as a scenic image. Compare the orange-pink sandbank in the Yale landscape with the corresponding passage of the whitish rock immediately above the weir in this picture, which is handled with tremendous energy and given form by a creeper created with a few stabs of a coarse brush. Gainsborough referred sardonically to his ability to produce 'a Flash in the Pan', and it was this kind of bravura work which astonished his contemporaries.

This is Gainsborough's most original portrait. Although most of the compositional elements, and to some extent the handling and colouring of this picture are not new to his work, the overall effect is, for from them he has produced an image of striking Romanticism. The crescent-shaped framing tree and bank upon which the subject sits are, for instance, essentially those which provided the setting for the powerful figure of *John Wilkinson* (page 105); the distant landscape is to be seen in scores of similar works, and the delicate, restless brushwork harks back to his earlier picture of Elizabeth with her sister (page 99). Perhaps it was that earlier work which gave him the idea of producing an image in which subject and setting were unified not only by colour and brushwork but by making the sitter a 'natural' figure, as much a part of her surroundings as the peasants who populated his landscapes. In *The Linley Sisters* the girls are civilized, urban people posing in an Arcadian setting; the landscape amplifies their innocence and beauty but they are quite obviously not of it. Their clothes are formal and expensive, for instance, and they have brought the trappings of their urban life – the guitar and music score – with them.

Thirteen years later, however, Elizabeth's dress is a Romanticized form of peasant woman's costume albeit of silk and muslin rather than wool and linen. And whereas in the earlier picture the landscape is suggested in a deliberately sketchy manner, with little depth, almost like a tapestry backcloth, here it is fully realized and the figure is shown to be intimately bound up with it. The wind that blows her hair also blows the branch above her head in a formal echo; the folds of her sash resemble the plant which grows along – almost into – the sides of her dress, and is delicately confused with the end of the gauze scarf. Her pose mimics the curve of tree and bank far more closely than the foursquare Mr Wilkinson. This is much closer to the idea of the 'dryad' – woman as nature spirit – than anything Gainsborough had produced before, yet there is absolutely nothing clas-

Mrs Brinsley Sheridan (née Linley)

Painted 1785–7
219.7 × 137 cm
National Gallery of Art, Washington DC

sical about the picture. It represents something beyond the idea of female 'sensibility', of delicacy and purity of feeling. This is a portrait of the Brontëan rather than the Austenian heroine, the woman of passion, in whom emotions are not refined by civilization but instead dominate and overthrow the restrictions of convention and social mores. It is not a 'respectable' image, and Elizabeth Sheridan was not a 'respectable' girl. She caused a scandal by eloping to France with Sheridan at the age of seventeen, only to be dragged home to Bath by her father, having a year earlier taken the unheard-of step of asking the man to whom she was formally engaged, a wealthy landowner called Walter Long, to release her, admitting she was in love with someone else.

This was one of the pictures which Gainsborough withdrew from the Royal Academy Summer Exhibition after a row with the Hanging Committee over the height at which his portraits should be placed. It is traditionally said to have been painted for King George III, with whom Gainsborough was at this time on very good terms, and on whose portrait, together with others of the Queen and their children, he had been working. Whether or not this was the case, it remained in Gainsborough's possession until his death. Owing to changing fashion Mrs Gainsborough was unable to sell it, even at the knock-down price of 200 guineas, and many years later it turned up in a sale of the collection of Gainsborough's friend Samuel Kilderbee.

There is no indication that the scene represented was intended to be the Mall. It is in fact derived from a painting by Watteau, *La Perspective*, which Gainsborough would have seen in an engraving. Watteau's picture shows an avenue leading up to a château, peopled with fashionably dressed women sitting or promenading. Using this format, Gainsborough has added more figures, and produced a picture which is quite unlike anything else in his oeuvre – or indeed that of any other British artist. Compositionally it is odd, having no central focus, a limited perspective, and almost no narrative interest. Not surprisingly – apart from a paean of praise from his good friend Sir Henry Bate-Dudley, and a somewhat ambiguous remark from Horace Walpole that it was 'all a-flutter like a lady's fan' – the picture aroused almost no interest or comment when it was exhibited in 1784 at Schomberg House, Gainsborough's home in Pall Mall. If it was done for the King, it may be that its curious design was on his instructions, or that it was intended to be just a decorative piece. There was another occasion on which Gainsborough hoped that the King would buy the picture he considered his masterpiece, *The Woodcutter*, as he asked for it to be shown to him at Windsor. Alas, the King did not buy it, and it was subsequently destroyed by fire, the sad

The Mall

Painted 1783
120.7 × 147 cm
The Frick Collection, New York

fate of a number of Gainsborough's works, including his portrait of David Garrick.

Gainsborough is known to have used dolls to pose the figures for this picture, as is suggested by their somewhat unnatural gait. Nevertheless, it has become one of his best-known pictures and, despite its uniqueness, it prefigures in the extreme delicacy of its handling and careful attention to overall 'tone' his portrait of Mrs and Mrs Hallett, *The Morning Walk* (page 131).

Although never completed, this is nevertheless one of Gainsborough's most satisfying late landscape compositions. The exceptionally ornate sunset is echoed in the curls of vegetation high on the cliff, and the bridge reflects the hump of the mountain on the left; the curved top of this mountain is given symmetry within the composition by the curve of the bank at lower right.

The inspiration for such an unusually mountainous scene may have been Gainsborough's tour of the Lake District with Samuel Kilderbee in 1783, but on that trip he produced sketches and watercolours only. Nevertheless his landscapes do become more turbulent and Romantic for a while thereafter.

It says much for Gainsborough's technique that we are able to appreciate the work almost as if it were a finished piece, so confident and crisp in his notation of the forms and the play of the light. Most artists might be expected to have left some passages tentatively suggested or scrubbed out; evidently Gainsborough knew almost exactly what he wanted to do. Why then was the picture not completed? By this stage in his career he could certainly have taken the time to work on such a project if he had wished; he was a very wealthy man and no longer at the beck and call of his clients. John Hayes* suggests that the cliffs on the right, which were built up as the picture progressed, dissatisfied him to such a degree that he simply abandoned it, but similar compositions, such as the towering rock in the Washington seascape (page 117) suggest that there may have been another reason. He was, as he confessed, 'full of fitts and starts'.

Mountain Landscape with Bridge

Painted c.1783–4
113 × 133.4 cm
National Gallery of Art, Washington DC

* *Gainsborough*, Tate Gallery catalogue, 1980, p. 152.

In the last decade of his life Gainsborough produced a number of 'fancy pictures' such as this one. These were a new development in British art, and Gainsborough was largely responsible for making them fashionable. The genre was derived from French painting, however, and this picture is clearly based on *The Broken Pitcher* by Jean-Baptiste Greuze (1725–1805), now in the Louvre (see page 39), of which Gainsborough would have seen an engraving. Whereas in Greuze's painting the girl gazes directly at the viewer and the broken pitcher serves as a metaphor for the loss of her virginity, Gainsborough has toned down this mawkishly sentimental element, removing the overt symbolism. The sitter was a girl whom Gainsborough had met by chance whilst out walking near Richmond; the puppy was her own. He also painted her in *The Girl with Pigs* (see page 38), for which he introduced a litter of piglets into Schomberg House for several days.

Although reaction to this particular picture was mixed – Hazlitt found it 'insipid' – it sold immediately for 200 guineas. Most of Gainsborough's contemporaries seem to have greeted his sentimental works with high praise; Reynolds, who bought *The Girl with Pigs*, called it the finest thing he had ever done.

Although the relationship of the present work to Greuze's original is quite close, it is not clear whether Gainsborough was motivated to work in this genre by his admiration for similar French art or whether the type was the logical extension of the kinds of figure he had been portraying in his landscape images. Not all of them are as saccharine as this; there is one of two boys watching a dog fight, which Gainsborough joked that he would follow up with the dogs watching the boys fighting. Many of them have a stronger narrative role, and prefigure the Victorian taste for such images. Not surprisingly, Gainsborough's fancy pictures remained popular throughout the century following his death, and this type of rustic picture enjoyed a revival at the end of the nineteenth century

The Cottage Girl

Painted 1785
174 × 124.5 cm
National Gallery of Ireland, Dublin

both in Britain and in France, for example in the work of Jules Bastien-Lepage (1848–84).

Although this now seems a highly contrived and over-sentimental image, it could be argued that this is to a large degree due to our over-exposure to mass-produced images of this kind. At the time it was first exhibited it evidently seemed a fresh and exciting picture, worthy of discussion on equal terms with the best of Gainsborough's landscape and portrait work. It is painted in a muted palette, without any great showmanship, and presents a bare minimum of pictorial elements in a straightforward way. Many later essays in the genre were considerably more contrived.

This is perhaps the best-known of Gainsborough's female portraits and it was considered to be the closest likeness of any of the many portraits which Sarah Siddons sat for. Once again Gainsborough broke with convention, for actors and actresses were usually shown in costume for their most famous roles, which in this case would have been Lady Macbeth. That was the way Reynolds chose to paint the actress; Gainsborough, however, has her in contemporary dress. His only advice to her on her arrival at his studio was to go out and buy a new hat, which she did. He also has the temerity to remark during the sitting, 'Madam, there is no end to your nose.'

The portrait was well received: 'A more exquisitly graceful, refined and harmonious picture I have never seen, the delicacy and sweetness, combined with the warmth and richness of the colouring, make it a very peculiar [special] picture', wrote Fanny Kemble, the actress's niece.* Over half a century later a French writer, Thoré-Burger, wrote of it:

*The great tragic actress who interpreted the passions with such energy and such feeling, and who felt them so strongly herself, is better portrayed in this simple half-length, in her day-dress, than in allegorical portraits or in character. . . . The portrait is so original, so individual, as a poetic expression of character, as a deliberate selection of pose, as bold colour and free handling, that it is like the work of no other painter. It is useless to search for parallels for there are none. Veronese a little – but no, it is a quite personal creation. This is genius.** *

For all its remarkable boldness and power, however, it is a strange work, quite unlike anything else Gainsborough did. The closest comparison in pose, a portrait of Anne, Countess of Radnor, done in 1778, is entirely different in both handling and expression. The pose itself is an uncomplicated one, and the red background curtain appears in a number of his studio portraits. It is most curious, however, that he chose to portray the actess with an almost sphinx-like gaze,

Mrs Siddons

Painted 1785
126.4 × 99.7 cm
The National Gallery, London

communicating nothing of her profession save her striking good looks. The drapery is handled with considerable élan, but less freely than in many portraits, and the fur muff is executed with extraordinary care, as is the wisp of lace which falls over it. Yet the sleeve of her right arm is clumsily done – one is tempted to speculate that his assistant Gainsborough Dupont was left to handle it – and that arm is awkwardly set, appearing rather longer than the left one. That being said, the picture has become the quintessential image of the eighteenth-century fashionable woman – strong, characterful and glamorous. From purely conventional elements Gainsborough has conjured a portrait of immense conviction and power.

*Quoted in Worman, *Thomas Gainsborough: a biography*, p. 120.

For many critics and commentators this is Gainsborough's greatest picture, a judgement with which it is hard to disagree. So many elements of his remarkably disparate work came together here that it is easy to see it as the culmination of his career, the point at which the various developments and experiments in his landscape and portrait work are resolved into an harmonious finale. It is, of course, a marriage portrait, and this seems apt, since it was with *Mrs and Mrs Andrews* (page 55) almost forty years earlier that he first gave notice of his peculiar talent, and first attempted to marry the genres of landscape and portraiture. One has only to compare the two pictures to realize the astonishing development his art has undergone over those years. If, in *Mrs and Mrs Andrews*, we are able to discern what for want of a better word we may call his 'genius', despite the limitations of his technique (limitations shown by most of his British contemporaries), it would have been impossible to pre-suppose from that picture his arrival at anything resembling *The Morning Walk*. Such complete stylistic transformation is probably unique in art.

Gainsborough has succeeded here in combining the atmospheric subtlety of portraits such as *Mrs Sheridan* (page 121) with the relaxed formality of more conventional works such as *John Wilkinson* (page 105). A certain degree of formality is necessary in a marriage portrait; the rhapsodic Romanticism of *Mrs Sheridan* would have been inappropriate. So, while Gainsborough has chosen a perfectly ordinary 'promenade' pose – as in *The Byam Family* (page 85), for example – and framed it with his usual overhanging tree and park-like vista, he has concentrated on unifying his subjects and their surroundings by his most subtle exercise in colour and handling. The brushwork is extremely light – no bravura short cuts here – with textures built up from repeated flicks of thin paint, and highlit with immense precision and delicacy. The complicated range of colour in Mrs Hallett's dress, from purplish-pink and grey in the

The Morning Walk

Painted 1785
236.2 × 179.1 cm
The National Gallery, London

---

shadow to pale apricot, is echoed in the sky behind and even in her husband's cravat. The landscape is also more precisely defined than in many comparable pictures, so that the effect of the subjects being posed in front of a backdrop is reduced. The poise of the figures is complete, and as John Hayes has pointed out,* the two compositional diagonals from the upper and lower left-hand side come together at exactly the point where Mrs Hallett's hand rests on her husband's arm, the true centre of the picture. It is a faultless performance, the quintessence of grace and urbanity.

* Gainsborough, Tate Gallery catalogue, 1980.

When Gainsborough first exhibited this work in his private exhibition of 1786 at Schomberg House, it lacked the figure of the woodman on the right, which was added the following year. The figure seems such a vital counterbalance to the rest of the composition that it is hard to imagine that he could have felt satisfied with the original version. The bright sleeve of the woodman's shirt forms one end of a diamond-shaped configuration of highlights on the horse, dog, walking child and the headband of the small girl in the cart.

The picture is painted in a considerably more firm and closely detailed manner than most of Gainsborough's late landscapes, and displays nothing of the interest in more ruggedly Romantic scenery that he had shown a few years earlier. The framing tree on the right is very crisply done, and instead of his usual feathery middleground trees, Gainsborough has painstakingly stippled the leaves of the small tree nearest the cart. And whereas the distant view and the left-hand framing trees are very similar to those in *The Morning Walk* (page 131), there is nothing of the misty, soft atmosphere of that only slightly earlier work. Nowhere is this sharpening of focus more apparent than in the cloudscape, easily the most naturalistic Gainsborough ever employed in his mature landscape work, a study of summer cumulus rather than an exercise in ornamentation. Here then, at last, we are able to discern something quite close to Constable's 'naturalistic' landscapes of the early 1800s.

The Market Cart

Painted 1786
184.2 × 153 cm
The National Gallery, London

This is the last of Gainsborough's six self-portraits which survive (not counting those with his wife and children), and is probably the one he was painting for his close friend, the musician Karl Friedrich Abel, who died before it could be completed. Gainsborough was now in his sixty-first year, but the portrait shows remarkably little change from earlier self-examinations and not a trace of creeping infirmity; the upright stance and piercing, sceptical gaze are those of a man half his age. It is handled with the great freedom which Gainsborough habitually employed latterly in intimate portraits intended for friends, such as that of de Loutherburg. The oval surround, however, is a device taken from his earliest work, which he had continued to use from time to time for small pictures. Although it appears sketchy, the picture is probably all but complete. A few months later Gainsborough discovered the symptoms of his own fatal illness.

Self-Portrait

Painted 1787
74.9 × 61 cm
Royal Academy of Arts, London

This picture, the last that Gainsborough completed, was intended as a companion piece to *The Market Cart* (page 133), although in style it is much less naturalistic. Where *The Woodcutter's Return* (page 101) is tentative and *The Cottage Door* (page 113) animated, here everything is serene. Although in many ways identical to *The Cottage Door*, here the compositional elements form an image of benevolent enfolding nature. The message is one of the rewards of honest toil, and a celebration of the simple pleasures of life – the latter something which Gainsborough himself apparently yearned to enjoy. He had his cottage near Richmond, but expressed a wish to retire 'to some sweet village' while still comparatively young; an acquaintance recorded how, when out riding, his gaze would soften and his conversation stall whenever he saw some particularly picturesque group of village buildings. Gainsborough must have known that such a retirement was impossible, however, for he was a man 'who knew everybody and everybody knew him'. It is not surprising, then, that he returned repeatedly to this idyllic rural scene in his work, and that when he suspected he was fatally ill (from the spring of 1788) he should round off the series with one of his warmest and most serene images of evening.

Cottage Door with Peasant Smoking

Painted 1788
195.6 × 157.5 cm
The Wight Art Gallery, Los Angeles

Most sources date this picture to the summer of 1788 when, working in increasing pain and for fewer hours each passing week, Gainsborough began what would have been his most ambitious work, his first and only venture into the painting of mythological subjects, the territory of the 'History Painters' and in particular of his greatest rival, Reynolds. Yet to start such a large and complex scene when terminally ill would have been surprising, and it may very well have been begun earlier. Hayes dates it to 1785. Gainsborough had always professed a dislike of classical subjects (this one is taken from Ovid's *Metamorphoses*) and had only occasionally attempted complicated groups of figures – and never the female nude. He also, untypically, made a considerable number of preliminary drawings and sketches, and what we see today is probably not the finalized composition. The figure of Actaeon the hunter who stumbles on Diana bathing, was altered several times, and in this version is shown at the moment when he is tranformed into a stag by the furious goddess.

Clearly it would have been a magnificent piece, and it seems from the amount of work Gainsborough managed to do on it that he truly intended to finish it. It may be that he felt that in order to seal his reputation he needed to demonstrate that he could turn his hand to History painting, still reckoned the highest form of art. Or perhaps he had already begun the picture before he fell ill, and had been intending to steer his career in a new direction; the signs are that demand for his landscapes was tailing off, partly because they were fantastically expensive. *Cottage Door with Peasant Smoking* (page 137) was priced at 500 guineas, and failed to sell. A decade after his death, the Prince of Wales purchased *Diana and Actaeon* for two pounds and three shillings. A few months before his death Gainsborough heard that his first great landscape *Cornard Wood* (page 53) had been sold. Forty years on, in its use of twin perspec-

Diana and Actaeon

Begun c.1785 (unfinished at death)
158.1 × 188 cm
Royal Collection, St James's Palace.
© Her Majesty the Queen

tives leading obliquely to left and to right, with the right-hand side in shadow and indicating the watercourse, and the centre marked by a tree, *Diana and Actaeon* echoes the structure of that early masterpiece 'in the schoolboy stile'.

CHRONOLOGY

1727
14 May – Baptized at the Independent Meeting House, Friars Street, Sudbury, Suffolk. Death of George I.

1739
Allan Ramsay returns to London from the Continent. Captain Coram opens the Foundling Hospital. Gainsborough possibly begins work on *Cornard Wood*.

1740
Gainsborough is sent to London and begins an apprenticeship in a silversmith's shop, learning engraving. Hogarth paints his portrait of *Captain Coram* for the Foundling Hospital. First public art exhibition is held in London, at the hospital.

c.1741–43
Gainsborough studies at St Martin's Lane Academy and meets Hayman, Gravelot and Hogarth.

c.1745
Gainsborough establishes a studio – probably in Hatton Garden. On a visit to Sudbury in this year or the next he meets Margaret Burr, illegitimate daughter of the Duke of Beaufort. Paints *Bumper*, probably his earliest surviving work.

1746
15 July – Marries Margaret Burr at Dr Keith's Mayfair Chapel, London.

c.1747
Possibly works with Hayman on decorations for the Vauxhall Gardens.

1748
The Trustees of the Foundling Hospital accept Gainsborough's gift of a painting of *The Charterhouse*. October 29 – Death of his father John. Birth of his daughter Mary. Moves to Friars Street, Sudbury. Paints (or finishes) *Cornard Wood*.

1752
Moves to 34 Foundation Street, Ipswich. Birth of second daughter Margaret. Meets Samuel and Mary Kilderbee.

1753
Joshua Reynolds settles in London and paints hugely influential portrait of *Commodore Keppel*, using pose of Apollo Belvedere. Gainsborough meets Philip Thicknesse.

1755
Gainsborough receives – via Joshua Kirby – his first London commission, for two 'chimney-piece' landscapes for the Duke of Bedford.

1758
Makes a working tour of houses in Buckinghamshire and Oxfordshire. He remarks in a letter that he has too much portrait work in Ipswich to be able to visit Colchester.

1759
October – Moves to Bath. Paints portrait of *Ann Ford*, which prefigures his mature portrait style.

1760
Accession of George III. Gainsborough meets Uvedale and Robert Price.

1761
Gainsborough shows at the first exhibition of the Society of Artists.

1762
Opens a bank account at Messrs C. Hoare & Co.

1763
Falls seriously ill for several weeks; a newspaper announces his death. Afterwards moves to Lansdowne Road, on the outskirts of Bath. He sends a landscape for exhibition at the Society of Artists for the first time.

1764
Death of William Hogarth.

1765
Hayman becomes President of the Society of Artists.

1766
Gainsborough moves to The Circus, Bath.

1768
Gainsborough is invited to become a founder member of the Royal Academy; Joshua Reynolds is first President.

1769
Exhibits at the first Royal Academy Exhibition.

1771
Zoffany paints Gainsborough's portrait. Gainsborough is charging 100 guineas for a full-length portrait, Reynolds 150 guineas. Gainsborough paints portrait of *The Linley Sisters*.

1772
His nephew Gainsborough Dupont becomes his first and only apprentice.

1773
Quarrels with the Hanging Committee of the Royal Academy.

1774
Refuses to exhibit at the Academy. Quarrels with Philip and Ann Thicknesse and moves to Schomberg House, Pall Mall, London. Elected to the Council of the Royal Academy.

1775
Sends nothing to the Academy. Decorates Bach and Abel's Music Rooms in Hanover Square. Meets Philip de Loutherburg.

1776
Sends nothing to the Academy.
Paints portrait of Johann Christian Bach.

1777

Shows *The Watering Place* and *The Hon. Mrs Graham* amongst other pictures at the Academy. Both rapturously received. Bate-Dudley becomes his champion in the press. First portraits of members of the Royal Family.

1780

Paints George III and Queen Charlotte. Mary Gainsborough marries Johann Christian Fischer.

1781

Makes his 'peep-show box'. Exhibits his first sea-pictures and his first 'fancy picture'.

1782

Tours the West Country with Samuel Kilderbee. Reynolds buys his *Girl with Pigs*.

1783

Tours the Lake District with Kilderbee.

1784

Withdraws his pictures from the Royal Academy exhibition and never shows there again. Sets up private show at Schomberg House. Death of Allan Ramsay; Reynolds becomes Principal Painter to the King. Gainsborough paints *The Harvest Waggon*.

1785

Paints Elizabeth, *Mrs Brinsley Sheridan* and *The Morning Walk*. Begins *Diana and Actaeon*, left unfinished at his death, his first classical subject.

1787

Death of his friend Karl Friedrich Abel.

1788

Spring – Paints *Peasant Smoking at the Cottage Door*. Falls ill in March with cancer. 2 August – Dies. Is buried at Kew, Surrey.

1789

Sale of his pictures at Schomberg House. Reynolds gives his Discourse on the work of Gainsborough at the Academy.

1792

Sale of further pictures at Christie's; prices fall sharply. Death of Sir Joshua Reynolds. Lawrence becomes Principal Painter to the King. Death of Philip Thicknesse; his memoirs published.

1797

Death of Gainsborough Dupont.

1799

Death of Margaret Burr Gainsborough.

1820

Death of Margaret Gainsborough.

1826

Death of Mary Gainsborough Fischer.

SELECT BIBLIOGRAPHY

ARMSTRONG, W. *Gainsborough and his place in English Art*, Heinemann, 1904.

BARRELL, J. *The Dark Side of Landscape*, Cambridge University Press, 1980.

BIRMINGHAM, A. *Landscape and Ideology*, Thames & Hudson, 1984.

CORRI, A. *The Search for Gainsborough*, Jonathan Cape, 1984.

DIBDIN, E. *Thomas Gainsborough*, Cassell, 1923.

FULCHER, G.W. *Life of Thomas Gainsborough*, Longman, 1856.

GATT, G. *Gainsborough*, Thames and Hudson, 1968.

GREIG, J. and MENPES, M. *Gainsborough*, A. & C. Black, 1909.

HAYES, J. *Gainsborough: Paintings and Drawings*, Phaidon, 1975.

HAYES, J. *Thomas Gainsborough*, Tate Gallery, 1980.

HAYES, J. *Landscape Paintings of Thomas Gainsborough* (2 vols), Sotheby, 1982.

JOHNSON, E.D.H. *Paintings of the British Social Scene*, Weidenfeld & Nicolson, 1986.

LINDSAY, J. *Thomas Gainsborough, his Life and Art*, Granada, 1981.

REYNOLDS, J. *Discourses on Art*, Collier, 1969.

SHAWE-TAYLOR, D. *The Georgians*, Barrie & Jenkins, 1990.

THOMPSON, E.P. *The Making of the English Working Class*, Penguin, 1963.

WATERHOUSE, E. *Painting in Britain 1530–1790*, Penguin, 1953.

WATERHOUSE, E. *Gainsborough*, Hulton, 1958/Spring Books, 1966.

WHITLEY, W.T. *Thomas Gainsborough*, Smith, Elder, 1923.

WILLIAMS, R. *The Country and the City*, Hogarth Press, 1985.

WILLIAMSON, G. *The Ingenious Mr Gainsborough*, Hale, 1972.

WOODALL, (ed.) *Letters of Thomas Gainsborough*, Cupid Press, 1963.

WOODHALL, M. *Thomas Gainsborough: his Life & Work*, Phoenix House, 1949.

WORMAN, I. *Thomas Gainsborough: a Biography*, Dalton, 1976.

LIST OF PLATES

49 *A View in Suffolk*, c.1746–7. Oil on canvas, 47 × 61 cm. National Gallery of Ireland, Dublin.

51 *Couple of a Bench (Conversation dans un parc)*, c.1746–7. Oil on canvas, 76.2 × 67.3 cm. Musée du Louvre, Paris.

53 *Gainsborough's Forest (Cornard Wood)*, c.1746–8. Oil on canvas, 121.9 × 154.9 cm. Reproduced by courtesy of the Trustees, The National Gallery, London.

55 *Portrait of Mr and Mrs Andrews*, c.1748–50. Oil on canvas, 69.8 × 119.4 cm. Reproduced by courtesy of the Trustees, The National Gallery, London.

57 *Portrait of Heneage Lloyd and his Sister*, c.1751–2. Oil on canvas, 64.1 × 80 cm. Reproduced by Permission of the Syndics of the Fitzwilliam Museum, Cambridge.

59 *Portrait of John Plampin*, c.1764–5. Oil on canvas, 50.2 × 60.3 cm. Reproduced by courtesy of the Trustees, The National Gallery, London.

61 *Coastal Scene with Country Cart (View near the Coast)*, c.1750–5. Oil on canvas, 81.2 × 107.7 cm. Ipswich Borough Council Museums & Galleries Collection (R1941–76).

63 *Extensive River Landscape with View of Cornard Village*, c.1753. Oil on canvas, 76.2 × 151.1 cm. National Gallery of Scotland, Edinburgh (NG2174).

65 *Woodcutter Courting a Milkmaid*, 1755. Oil on canvas, 106.7 × 128.2 cm. By kind permission of the Marquess of Tavistock, and the Trustees of the Bedford Estates.

67 *Portrait of Mrs John Kirby (née Alice Brown)*, c.1755. Oil on canvas, 75.8 × 62.9 cm. Reproduced by Permission of the Syndics of the Fitzwilliam Museum, Cambridge.

69 *The Painter's Daughters chasing a Butterfly*, 1755–6. Oil on canvas, 113.7 × 104.8 cm. Reproduced by courtesy of the Trustees, The National Gallery, London.

71 *Portrait of The Reverend Richard Canning*, 1757. Oil on canvas, 76.2 × 63.5 cm. Ipswich Borough Council Museums & Galleries Collection (R1958–136).

73 *Portrait of Mrs Samuel Kilderbee (née Mary Wayth)*, 1757. Oil on canvas, 73 × 60 cm. Ipswich Borough Council Museums & Galleries (R1959–130).

75 *The Painter's Daughters with a Cat*, c.1758–60. Oil on canvas, 75.6 × 62.9 cm. Reproduced by courtesy of the Trustees, The National Gallery, London.

77 *Portrait of Mrs Philip Thicknesse*, date. Oil on canvas, 197.1 × 135 cm. Cincinnati Art Museum, Bequest of Mary M. Emery, (1927.396).

79 *Portrait of Uvedale Tomkins Price*, c.1760. Oil on canvas, 124.1 × 99.1 cm. Staatsgemäldesammlungen, Munich.

81 *A Grand Landscape*, c.1763. Oil on canvas, 146.1 × 157.5 cm. Worcester Art Museum, Worcester, Massachusetts.

83 *Portrait of General James Johnston*, c.1763–4. Oil on canvas, 206 × 141 cm. National Gallery of Ireland, Dublin.

85 *Portrait of The Byam Family*, c.1764. Oil on canvas, 248.9 × 238.8 cm. Marlborough College, Wiltshire.

87 *Wooded Landscape with Country Waggon, Milkmaid and Drover*, 1766. Oil on canvas, 144 × 119.4 cm. Reproduced by kind permission of a private collector.

89 *The Harvest Waggon*, 1767. Oil on canvas, 120.5 × 144.7 cm. The Barber Institute of Fine Arts, The University of Birmingham.

91 *Portrait of John Campbell, 4th Duke of Argyll*, c.1768. Oil on canvas, 235 × 154 cm. Scottish National Portrait Gallery, Edinburgh (PG1596).

93 *Portrait of Mary, Duchess of Montagu*, c.1768. Oil on canvas, 74.9 × 61.6 cm. Reproduced by kind permission of the Duke of Buccleuch and Queensberry, Bowhill.

95 *View near Kings Bromley on Trent*, c.1768–71. Oil on canvas, 117.5 × 168.3 cm. Philadelphia Museum of Art: William L. Elkins Collection (E'24-3-5).

97 *Portrait of Jonathan Buttall ('The Blue Boy')*, c.1770. Oil

on canvas, 177.8 × 121.9 cm. The Huntingdon Art Collections, San Marino.

99 *Portrait of The Linley Sisters (Mrs Sheridan and Mrs Tickell)*, c.1772. Oil on canvas, 199 × 153.1 cm. By permission of the Governors of Dulwich Picture Gallery.

101 *Wooded Landscape with Family Group outside the Cottage ('The Woodcutter's Return')*, c.1772–3. Oil on canvas, 146 × 120.6 cm. Reproduced by kind permission of His Grace the Duke of Rutland.

103 *A Mountain Valley with Rustic Figures, a Shepherd and Sheep, and a Distant Village and Mountains*, c.1773–7. Oil on canvas, 122 × 149 cm. Yale Center for British Art, Paul Mellon Collection (B1981.25.295).

105 *Portrait of John Wilkinson*, c.1775. Oil on canvas, 234 × 145 cm. Staatliche Museen zu Berlin © 1992 Bildarchiv Kulturbesitz, Berlin.

107 *Portrait of the Hon. Mrs Graham*, c.1775–7. Oil on canvas, 237 × 154 cm. National Gallery of Scotland, Edinburgh.

109 *Portrait of Hon Frances Duncombe*, c.1777. Oil on canvas, 233.7 × 154.9 cm. Copyright The Frick Collection, New York.

111 *Portrait of Mrs Gainsborough*, 1778. Oil on canvas, 76.6 × 63.8 cm. Courtauld Institute Galleries, London (Courtauld gift 1932).

113 *The Cottage Door*, c.1780. Oil on canvas, 147.3 × 119.4 cm. The Huntingdon Art Collections, San Marino.

115 *Portrait of Johann Christian Fischer*, 1780. Oil on canvas, 228.6 × 150.5 cm. Royal Collection, St James's Palace. © Her Majesty the Queen.

117 *Seashore with Fishermen*, c.1781–2. Oil on canvas, 102.2 × 127.9 cm. National Gallery of Art, Washington, DC, Ailsa Mellon Bruce Collection (1970.17.121(2493))..

119 *Rocky Landscape*, 1783. Oil on canvas, 119.4 × 147.3 cm. National Gallery of Scotland, Edinburgh (2253).

121 *Portrait of Mrs Brinsley Sheridan (née Linley)*, 1785–7. Oil on canvas, 219.7 × 137 cm. National Gallery of Art, Washington DC, Andrew W. Mellon Collection (1937.1.92(92)).

123 *The Mall*, 1783. Oil on canvas, 120.6 × 147 cm. Copyright The Frick Collection, New York.

125 *Mountain Landscape with Bridge*, c.1783–4. Oil on linen canvas, 113 × 133.4 cm. National Gallery of Art, Washington DC, Andrew W. Mellon Collection (1937.1.107(107)).

127 *The Cottage Girl*, 1785. Oil on canvas, 174 × 124.5 cm. National Gallery of Ireland, Dublin (Beit Collection).

129 *Portrait of Mrs Siddons*, 1785. Oil on canvas, 126.4 × 99.7 cm. Reproduced by courtesy of the Trustees, The National Gallery, London.

131 *The Morning Walk*, 1785. Oil on canvas, 236.2 × 179.1 cm. Reproduced by courtesy of the Trustees, The National Gallery, London.

133 *The Market Cart*, 1786. Oil on canvas, 184.2 × 153 cm. Reproduced by courtesy of the Trustees, The National Gallery, London.

135 *Self-Portrait*, 1787. Oil on canvas, 74.9 × 61 cm. Royal Academy of Arts, London.

137 *Cottage Door with Peasant Smoking*, 1788. Oil on canvas, 195.6 × 157.7 cm. Collection of the Wight Art Gallery, University of California, Los Angeles, Gift of Mrs James Kennedy.

139 *Diana and Actaeon*, c.1785 (unfinished at death). Oil on canvas, 158.1 × 188 cm. Royal Collection, St James's Palace. © Her Majesty the Queen.

PHOTOGRAPHIC ACKNOWLEDGEMENTS

Kunstdia-Archiv Artothek, Munich 79; Angelo Hornak 45; Lewis Photos Ltd, London 34; Réunion des musées nationaux, Paris 51; John Webb 47